THE DREAM WHISPERER

THE DREAM WHISPERER

Unlock the Power of Your Dreams

Davina MacKail

HAY HOUSE

HAY HOUSE

Australia • Canada • Hong Kong • India
South Africa • United Kingdom • United States

First published and distributed in the United Kingdom by:
Hay House UK Ltd, 292B Kensal Rd, London W10 5BE. Tel.: (44) 20 8962 1230;
Fax: (44) 20 8962 1239. www.hayhouse.co.uk

Published and distributed in the United States of America by:
Hay House, Inc., PO Box 5100, Carlsbad, CA 92018-5100. Tel.: (1) 760 431 7695 or
(800) 654 5126; Fax: (1) 760 431 6948 or (800) 650 5115. www.hayhouse.com

Published and distributed in Australia by:
Hay House Australia Ltd, 18/36 Ralph St, Alexandria NSW 2015.
Tel.: (61) 2 9669 4299; Fax: (61) 2 9669 4144. www.hayhouse.com.au

Published and distributed in the Republic of South Africa by:
Hay House SA (Pty), Ltd, PO Box 990, Witkoppen 2068. Tel./Fax: (27) 11 467 8904.
www.hayhouse.co.za

Published and distributed in India by:
Hay House Publishers India, Muskaan Complex, Plot No.3, B-2, Vasant Kunj,
New Delhi – 110 070. Tel.: (91) 11 4176 1620; Fax: (91) 11 4176 1630.
www.hayhouse.co.in

Distributed in Canada by:
Raincoast, 9050 Shaughnessy St, Vancouver, BC V6P 6E5. Tel.: (1) 604 323 7100;
Fax: (1) 604 323 2600

© Davina MacKail, 2010

A catalogue record for this book is available from the British Library.

Martin Taylor song lyrics on p.188 reprinted with kind permission of
P3 Music and Topic Records.

Georgie Fame song lyrics on p.233 reprinted with kind permission of
Musichouse (EMI Music Publishing).

ISBN 978-1-84850-196-6

Printed in the UK by CPI William Clowes Ltd, Beccles, NR34 7TL.

This paper is manufactured from material sourced from forests certified according to
strict environmental, social and economical standards.

This book is dedicated to Guy, the man of my dreams and my wonderful mum, for her eternal love and support

THE DREAM WHISPERER

Dreams are in the dawning, no beginning or end.
The unknowable knowing of all that is.
This treasury of sweetness holds the key,
unlocking the mystery of the one reality.
A glorious, unnameable knowing.
Unfathomable connection; a heavenly selection.

Emptiness whispers in the morning.
Universes conquered, galaxies yawning.
Wide open chasms of the mind.
The desire, the yearning; the realization
of the whispered dream inside.
Bathe in the eternal embrace, surrendering
to that state of grace.

The enormous nothing where everything resides.
Where time has no meaning, past and future collide,
yet the action is always ours to decide.
Consciousness exploding, rain falling
and the slow, sweet whisper of the breath.
Spaces expanding, holographic universes unfolding;
flowing in.

Silently it comes, this voice of dreams
from that place where we cannot
be killed or die. Where truth lies,
entangled in the whispers of the mind.
Words are not the meaning, it's the spaces in between.
Where time is lost, love is found, and the healing is profound.

Contents

Acknowledgements   x

Introduction   xi

Chapter One: Very Briefly...   1

Chapter Two: To Sleep Is to Dream   17

Chapter Three: The Dream Gym   45

Chapter Four: Mind the Gap   65

Chapter Five: Symbol and Metaphor   85

Chapter Six: Universal Energy   107

Chapter Seven: Playing the Time Game   133

Chapter Eight: You're Not Alone   155

Chapter Nine: Your New Best Friends   181

Chapter Ten: Dealing with Fear   205

Chapter Eleven: Unlock your Inner Einstein   225

Afterword   245

Appendix : Dream Symbols – Some Interpretations   249

Further Reading and Resources   257

Acknowledgements

There are many people I would like to thank for this book, including all the hidden heroes who made up the publishing team, from designers, to typesetters, to proofreaders, to publicists and assistants. Thank you to Tony Fitzpatrick for opening all the doors, and to Richard Bellars, coach extraordinaire, for blasting me through my writer's block allowing this book to begin. Very special thanks to Matthew Wright, for your generous encouragement – thanks to you, this book got written! Thank you to Michelle Pilley for your initial instinct and faith in this idea and, of course, all the team at Hay House UK, for your endless enthusiasm and support. I couldn't have dreamed up better publishers! I feel blessed that our paths have crossed. Thank you to Lizzie Hutchins for your great advice and excellent attention to detail during the edit. Endless thanks and blessings to my dearest friends Carl Hyatt, Ruth Needham, Bharti Mehta, Carla Miles and Suzie Shaw – I truly couldn't have done it without you guys, thank you for all your practical support and emotional encouragement. Special thanks to Derian Parsad and Liz Adams for your wonderful assistance on book-related matters, and Mary Cross for your speedy transcriptions. For keeping mind, body and soul together, special thanks go to June O'Reilly, Jean Robinson, all at Bikram Yoga, Chiswick, my mastermind circle group and my Venus sisters. Eternal gratitude to Mum and Paul, thank you for feeding me and providing a perfect writing retreat. Far too many thank you's to Guy, my wonderful husband, for everything that you are and all your love, and an extended thank you to all my other family and friends who have loved and encouraged me along the way – you know who you are!

My deep gratitude to all those named and unnamed whose dreams have been included. Your stories are the soul of this book and I thank each of you for sharing your dream adventures with me.

And finally thank you to all my teachers, old and new, who continue to encourage, support and inspire me to see the bigger picture and think outside the box; and grateful thanks to life itself, the greatest teacher, and to dreamers everywhere for continuing to believe in your dreams.

Introduction

'I am the vehicle and all
I need are my dreams.'

Davina MacKail

Why is it that every night, whilst we sleep, we are completely paralysed, fully sexually stimulated, flooded with creative chemicals and forced to watch incomprehensible movies in our mind?

This is the world of our dreams. Every sleep of our life presents a unique opportunity to access this fantastical, mystical world where quite literally anything could happen and generally does. Galaxies of extraordinary landscapes unfold, improbable events become commonplace, bizarre creatures are manifested, time and space become whimsical playthings and every emotion known to us is invoked, from anger to terror to ecstasy to joy and all those in between.

From earliest times dreams have fascinated us, and for good reason. They offer moments of truth that reveal something of ourselves. We can lie whilst awake, but we can't fake our dreams.

Consider for a moment what it would be like to know yourself deeply – to know how to solve your problems and heal yourself. Wouldn't that allow you to be more of who you are, to do more of what you want to do and have more of what you want to have? That's the power of your dreams.

The definitive purpose of dreaming remains one of the great unsolved mysteries. The worlds of science and psychology both have their views, but no one has the absolute answer as to whether dreams are purely a physiological or a psychological necessity. They are many things, often all at once. But science has proven that they are ways of seeking solutions, maintaining our mental health, improving performance and sustaining sleep.

From my own experience I believe dreams play a more fundamental role in our lives than we have thus far given them credit for. For me, their purpose is threefold: they are a process of reorganization of the self, a means to understanding who we truly are and an infinite source of creativity and inspiration.

Have you ever wondered who you truly are? Do you want to tap into the extraordinary resources of energy within you? Do you want to live an inspired life? A fulfilled life? Do you want to know how to take the next steps? Your dreams can show you how.

Perhaps it is their bizarre and elusive nature that makes us question their use. Or the oft-quoted refrain 'Oh, but I never remember my dreams' that leads us to leave this unique personal resource mostly untapped. Only when we are startled awake by a dream so vivid and powerful it cannot be ignored do we ponder its meaning or delight in telling our friends and family in the secret hope that they may be able to throw some light on this seemingly nonsensical night-time drama.

Some people do more than relate their dreams to others – they act on them. Einstein's theory of relativity, Elias Howe's sewing machine and Paul McCartney's 'Yesterday' all came from dreams. Now it's your turn to discover your dream genius. This book gives you step-by-step instructions on how to unlock the power of your dreaming mind, taking you on the adventure of a lifetime. It is a book to dip into and ponder as you become engaged with your night-time whisperings. Each chapter will explore exercises for enhancing the dream experience and throughout the book there will be an emphasis on simple but effective techniques to allow you to get to grips with the interpretation of your own dreams.

Peppered throughout are wonderful examples of dreams from personalities who are well respected in their particular field of endeavour. I am truly grateful for all those who have allowed their dreams to be included. My intention is for you to be inspired by these stories and through them to see the benefit of discovering the multi-layered dimensions of your own dreams.

This book is designed to whisper to your dreaming mind, inviting it to become awake. Give yourself permission to let go into the words and let them float over you as you read. This will assist you in bridging the gap between your unconscious and conscious minds.

When we go to sleep at night we may think we have absolutely no control over the visions that will unfold before our eyes. Yet, as we will discover, there is an extraordinary intelligence present, an intelligence that directs our nocturnal dramas. This nebulous being is the Dream Whisperer. This is the commanding voice that directs our dreaming attention, always navigating us towards our individual truth. It is the energy that chooses to ferry our inner knowing across the bridge from our unconscious to our conscious awareness. During the night we are mere playthings to the Dream Whisperer. It can leave us screaming, sweating, laughing, erotically satisfied and much more besides. It is a voice in all of us, encouraging and cajoling us towards wholeness and the understanding that we are so much more than we can possibly imagine. I invite you to reconnect to the magic of your inner being, that small whispering voice of your dreams, to experience the wonder of daily miracles in your life.

A conscious understanding of what shows up in your dreams is essential to making them a powerful resource. You can then use that information to engage with your inner genius proactively whilst awake and program your mind more effectively whilst asleep. You will become your own private detective, searching your dreams for clues to your own way forward. Armed with this knowledge, you can make choices that can range from the subtle to the dramatic to improve your current situation and manifest the life you desire. If you can imagine it, you can become it.

Whatever we're searching for, our dreams hold the key. We don't even have to be asleep! We can access dream solutions whilst awake, and I will show you how. My intention in these pages is to fire your imagination and curiosity and help you to reconnect to your dreams.

My experiences as a shaman and hypnotist have given me a unique insight into the way dreams can be analysed and processed. The shamans of South America and many others believe we dream our world into being. For them, the world we live in is a direct result of our consensual dreaming. To change our reality we need to be brave enough to dream new dreams. This book will lead you through the process of unlocking the secrets of your inner psyche and using what you learn to transform your daily life.

Through the inspiration of my own dreams I have understood many things that my conscious mind was unable to provide solutions for. I have found answers to problems at work, discovered how to resolve difficult relationships and been alerted to health issues that needed addressing. However, perhaps the greatest gift my dreaming has given me to date is my father. One morning I woke from a deep dream with two simultaneous thoughts: 'I'm going to find my father and I'm going to resign my syndicated astrological column.' These events didn't appear to be related. I was 38 years old and my father had never known of my existence, so he wasn't going to come and find me. I only knew three facts about him: his name, nationality and star sign, Gemini. Without the internet, it would have been a hopeless task. But with this wonderful facility I was able to do a people search of the whole of America. It returned eleven addresses connected with his name and I wrote the same letter to all of them, emphasizing I wasn't after their money. Two weeks later, I found him. He emailed me from Paradise Valley, Arizona, on the day that my last astrological prediction was printed. I found out much later he's not a Gemini at all, he's a Libran. I wrote this prediction for Libra the week I found him:

So you thought it was all sorted, did you? Well, the sky has some fascinating news for you this week, the sort of news that will make your hair stand on end when you first hear it but then, when you've sat and digested the bombshell, you will begin to smile and then laugh very gleefully indeed.

It almost convinced my sceptical father to believe in astrology! I travelled to Arizona two months later to meet him for the first time. I'm not sure what other travellers at the airport thought when faced with the enormous sign he was holding, which simply said, 'Hi, Davina, it's Dad' – not a message you see every day! And not strictly necessary – you wouldn't need a DNA test to see we're related. The relationship developed and two years later he walked me down the aisle on my wedding day. Maybe that's why I'd had to wait so long before meeting a man I wanted to marry!

I also met my husband in a dream – well, his eyes anyway. This dream ended with a powerful close-up of a man's face. I couldn't see other facial details, just the eyes staring at me, and I felt overwhelming love as I looked into them. When I first met my future husband, I didn't recognize his eyes as those in my dream and we were friends for a long while. Then one evening he looked at me and those exact eyes appeared, and the rest, as they say, is history!

My dreams' guidance and humour continue to provide healing and solutions and I look forward to the creative input the Dream Whisperer brings each night...

Knowing that we have a potential dream genius inside us is a powerful and exciting concept. It gives us a sense of purpose. It allows us to believe that we can co-create a different waking reality, that we can take charge of our future. Best of all, regardless of personal circumstances, we need nothing more than we already have. In terms of creative potential we are indeed all born equal and the power lies within our dreaming mind.

Ideas are the currency of true success – not money, not education, not parenting, not luck, but ideas. Look around. Pretty much everything you can see only exists because someone had the idea in the first place. Our ideas come from our dreams and they hold the key to our success.

So, whilst it is helpful to interpret a dream and discover a fascinating insight into what makes us tick, it can be life-changing to actively seek answers to our problems by setting our dreams to work for us. The brain is highly motivated and solution driven during dream sleep. It is also flooded with the body's most potent cocktail of creative chemicals – optimum conditions for a genius moment! How many more Einsteins and Nobel Prize winners live amongst us, unrecognized, because we fail to pay attention to the messages of our dreams?

In ancient times, it was very different. Dreams were revered and honoured. Entire temples were constructed in the pursuit of healing dreams. We'll look at how we can replicate some of these methods today. In my work healing houses, I have consciously used dreams to assist me in getting the best results for my clients. As will be discussed further in Chapter Nine, these dreams have always proved to be significant and relevant to the healing work required, to the point where I no longer doubt their truth and entirely trust their superior wisdom. I hope this book inspires you to do the same with your own dreams.

I encourage you to make friends with your dreams, especially the terrifying ones. These are like diamonds – more precious for the intense pressure required to produce their brilliance.

Dreams of all kinds are remarkably responsive to any attention we give them. They want to be heard – all we need to do is listen! Simply choosing to own this book and browsing through it at random will immediately increase your ability to recall dreams clearly. You can also use it as a dream oracle. Ponder your dream or dream question. Close your eyes, turn the book upside down and round about and then open it where you feel called and read what is on that page. It may give you a technique to use for dream analysis or something that provokes a dream response, but whatever you've asked, there will be a clue on the page that relates to your question – guaranteed! I use this process a lot with the books in my library. It is an easy and excellent way of tapping into our unconscious resources.

Alternatively, you can read a section of the book before sleeping to trigger a dream. There are so many ways to use it. It offers a programme of exercises that will benefit anyone who wants to realize their true potential. Every technique is here because I have tested it and it works. As with anything worthwhile in life, you will get out of it what you put in, in terms of effort and commitment. But dreams truly are the gateway to your glorious self and the most potent form of personal therapy available, besides being completely free! So I encourage you to give this gift to yourself by following the recommendations given.

No dream dictionary is included here, as I believe the only person who can truly interpret your dreams is you. There are many dictionaries out there to get you started, if you feel you need them. But be wary and use them sparingly, as each person will have a unique perspective on every symbol. Two people dreaming of a river, for example, will have very different interpretations, due to the detail of their particular dream and their individual associations with the concept of a river. In dreams, details are important! They are one of the keys that help us understand why and how a particular image has shown up for us and what it means in relation to our current life experience. Rarely are dreams as simple as dream dictionaries make out – they are a treasure trove of insights into our true and miraculous nature, and one that will deeply reward our efforts to penetrate their meaning.

The deliciousness of dreams is that they respond in such organic ways. They come and go throughout our life.

Sometimes we record them, sometimes we don't. Some we'll always remember, however many years ago we dreamed them, and others are gone in a flash, leaving their whispered memory nagging at the edges of our mind. But whatever remains with us is useful in some manner, offering up some nugget of truth for inspection and reflection.

This is especially valuable, for in our desperation to gain control and certainty in an uncertain world we have taken our rational thinking to its limits and thereby lost our ability to perceive other energies, other dimensions, other realms of experience. Engaging with our dreaming selves will reawaken us to ourselves. It will help us to uncover our inner wholeness. There is a pull within humanity as old as time itself to seek this out, though we don't always recognize it for what it is. In fact we often mistake it as a case of depression or general dissatisfaction with life or a nagging feeling that something's missing. But our dreams can set us on the path to wholeness and healing. They are a gift we were all born with, one that is innately ours. One that will support us, feed us and grow with us.

My greatest wish is to invoke a renewed passion for dreaming. I am deeply committed to waking us up to our own magnificence, and dreams are an essential ingredient in that process. Until we understand our own hidden depths, we are but half awake. Now is the time to awaken fully to who we are and create a life of passion, purpose and joy.

CHAPTER ONE

Very Briefly...

The History and Science of Sleep

'If you want to understand human nature, the human mind, what makes us tick, you need to look at dreams.'

Professor McNamara, Boston University School of Medicine, *Horizon*, BBC2, 10.02.09

The Briefest History of Sleep

Much has been written about the history of dreams and there are plenty of books to explore on the subject if you'd like to delve more deeply. For our purposes, I'm simply summing up the timeline of how our theories on dreams have developed, as it will help you engage and connect with this ancient commodity and understand how the symbolic language of the unconscious was discovered.

The Ancient World

The earliest recorded dreams are found in materials dating back around 5,000 years. In the Bible, Jacob, Joseph, Nebuchadnezzar and Solomon are all visited by God or a divine prophet in their dreams. Moreover, those dreams were seen as revelatory in nature and guided those men's future decisions. The Talmud also contains masses of references to dreams. The Hebrews, Egyptians, Mesopotamians, Chinese and many more ancient cultures all believed in the extraordinary power of dreams. In Japan, both Shinto and Buddhist temples practised the art of dream incubation, programming the mind to dream on a specific topic.

In ancient times dreams were seen as direct messages from gods and spirits or were revered as prophecies that needed to be understood and acted on, as in the famous biblical story of Jacob and the Pharaoh of Egypt, who had a dream that indicated seven years of feast followed by seven years of famine.

It was accepted lore that the dreams of kings had the power to influence whole nations. In the classical story of King Gilgamesh, he reported his dreams to his mother. She interpreted them and changed the course of history, as the king used the information to guide his future actions.

The Dark Ages

Sadly, dreams were forgotten in the West as the Roman Empire gave way to the Dark Ages. We lost our interest in gods and prophetic visions as Christianity became mainstream and our thinking turned towards the rational, culminating in the Newtonian view of the world that took hold in the late seventeenth century.

The only peoples who have remained in touch with their dream lives throughout recorded history are indigenous shamanic cultures. They have always used dreams. However, at some point in history most of these peoples have been persecuted and forced to retreat and hide away their esoteric wisdom. Only relatively recently has this re-emerged, as interest in these ancient cultures has grown.

Shamans have a very practical attitude towards dreaming. They're the original pragmatists; they use what's readily available to them and dreams are a daily free resource, so inevitably they're going to tap into them. They use them for diagnosis, guidance, tribal decisions, prophecy and healing amongst other things. A shamanic healer will dream on behalf of somebody in the community to gain an insight into their presenting problem. Their way of communicating this message might seem alien to our western minds – they might deem the problem to relate to an ancestral issue or a malevolent spirit that has inhabited the patient's being, for example – but their advice will usually be effective for all that.

Interestingly, shamans believe that what we perceive as reality is actually a consensual dream. They say we are all dreaming this reality into being – and that it isn't reality at all, it's just an illusion.

Freud

In the West, the next big phase of dream interpretation, which has continued to the present day, began with Freud, the father of psychoanalysis, at the end of the nineteenth century. He put dreams back on the mainstream agenda as 'the royal road to the unconscious', culminating in his seminal work, *The Interpretation of Dreams*, originally published in 1900.

Freud was the first to give credence to the symbolic nature of the unconscious. He postulated that dreams had a psychological impact on us and were worth investigating in terms of understanding ourselves. More specifically, he claimed they could be understood through analysing their symbolism. His work was revolutionary in an age that favoured the positivist ideas of science over the superstitious and intangible. Freud himself attempted to bridge this gap with his work on dreams and proved through the analysis of hundreds of patients that a unified explanation of dreams was possible.

Freud thought dreams could be hard for the conscious mind to understand because they were all repressed desires, tendencies that people didn't really want to admit that they had. He believed the meanings were concealed in obscure symbolism to prevent people from acting out these repressed fantasies. He also believed they were predominantly sexual in nature. In fact he could make a sexual association for every dream symbol imaginable. For example, walking upstairs in a dream would represent an erection. As we're fully sexually stimulated during dreaming sleep, perhaps there's something to be said for this theory! But of course Freud was living in an era where any outward expression of sexuality was taboo, and what is repressed in our external world seems to have a habit of appearing in our dreamtime as a way of balancing our psyche.

Whilst modern science and psychology have now left the ideas of Freud behind in terms of understanding the meaning of dreams, his legacy lives on and an aspect of his dream-interpretation techniques, namely free association, is as useful today as it ever was.

Jung

Freud's most promising student, Carl Jung, was the second pioneer of modern dream understanding. He eventually moved away from Freud and developed his own dream theory.

For Jung, all dreams were about the process of individuation – bringing us back to wholeness. He believed we would always dream about the part of ourselves that we hadn't given expression to in the waking world. It is the need of the unconscious mind to bring to light the real self, the true self, and Jung realized that our dreaming mind did this through archetypes, symbolic forms and metaphoric stories. He believed, as do I, that recurring dreams were about issues we'd neglected and were showing up repeatedly to demand attention. He saw us all steeped in the soup of what he termed the 'collective unconscious'. When we actually understand this unconscious through our dream symbols, we can bring it to conscious awareness and lead more balanced, reasonable lives. For Jung, this was the purpose of dreaming.

After Jung came many other psychologists, including Adler, Frederick Perls, Calvin Hall, Erickson, Maslow, Hartmann and Piotrowski, who believed that dreams had the purpose of maintaining mental health and interpersonal relationships and could be interpreted through their symbolic images, though each had their own unique take on this broad concept.

The Briefest Science of Sleep

Extraordinarily, the scientific world didn't get involved in studying dreams until the 1950s. Since then the jury has been out on what the function of a dream really is, though new studies are being conducted all the time. So far, science views dreaming as predominantly a physiological process and considers there is no merit to be gained from analysing dream content. From this perspective, dreams are purely a way of reorganizing the memories and the data we didn't have time to process during the day. They're also involved in our learning and growth mechanisms.

I would suggest that any one of us who's experienced a significant dream that we just *know* means something would disagree with that cold biological explanation. Views are in fact changing in the scientific community as more information comes to light, and psychologists still maintain that dreams are symbolic messages from our unconscious and believe their interpretation has meaning and therapeutic benefit.

I suspect the truth is that dreams are memories, data, learning, growth, messages – and more.

Let's now take a quick look at the physiology of dreaming in order to understand how to work our dreaming muscles to best effect.

Sleep Cycles

Dreaming happens in cycles. We need to understand how these work in order to know how the quality of our sleep will affect our dreams. Then we can utilize the different stages of sleep to program our dreaming mind and access our potential.

Since the 1950s and the advent of sleep laboratories, science has added considerably to our understanding of the dreaming mind and in particular the sleep cycle. It has revealed that the ultradian sleep cycle rotates approximately every 90 minutes throughout the night. Within this, there are five stages of sleep.

The first two stages are what is known as NREM sleep (non-rapid eye movement sleep). Stage one is a very light sleep. At this point we're just drifting off. We're beginning to slow down our breathing, but we're not fully asleep. If somebody disturbed us, we'd wake from this stage very quickly. It's a very light trance state, the precursor to sleep, and is excellent for actively engaging with our dreaming mind. We'll come back to this shortly. Stage two is a slight deepening of stage one.

Stages three and four are also NREM states. We are now entering what's known as slow-wave sleep. This is the restorative part of sleep, where the body repairs itself on a cellular level. We need this stage to awaken feeling refreshed and as though we've had a good night's sleep. During these stages our heartbeat slows down, as does our breathing. It's very difficult to be woken up from this stage. We're truly 'out for the count'.

The last stage, stage five, is when we go into REM sleep (rapid eye movement sleep), commonly known as dream sleep. This is when the majority of our dreaming takes place.

During an average night's sleep we cycle through these stages around four to five times. REM sleep increases as the night wears on. During the first cycle we get about ten minutes of it. By the time we reach the morning cycle this has increased to around 45 minutes to an hour. If we wake

up during one of these REM cycles we tend to have recall of
our dreams – which explains why we're much more likely to
remember our dreams in the morning, as we're in dream sleep
for a lot longer then.

From work done in sleep labs there is evidence to suggest
that we do also dream in the earlier NREM phases of sleep,
though these dreams appear less dramatic. When people
are woken during these earlier phases, their dreams tend to
contain mundane information directly related to recent events
in their life – what Freud dubbed 'day residue' dreams. At this
stage we are simply processing our daily life. The juicy stuff,
the blockbuster dreams, tends to come in the REM phase.

The Phenomenon of REM Sleep

When we enter REM sleep, our physiology changes
dramatically. Our brain becomes incredibly active, as if
we were awake but in a different way. Our heartbeat and
breathing rate increase. All our voluntary muscles are
paralyzed, which is just as well, as if they weren't we
would be out there acting out our dreams – which is a pretty
terrifying thought!

All big-brained mammals that we're aware of dream, or
have periods of REM sleep anyway. *What* they dream, we
don't obviously know – although sometimes actions speak
louder than words. The French scientist Michel Jouvet
experimented with severing the nerves that created sleep
paralysis in cats and observed what happened when they slept.
In their dreaming state, the cats got up and started stalking,
killing and eating imaginary prey. When the scientists lured
them with normal cat food, they completely ignored it. They
were absolutely acting out their dreams and those dreams
seemed to be similar to their waking reality.

Without having to go to such extreme lengths, I'm sure any
dog owner would tell you their pet dreams heartily of chasing
rabbits across fields. There are wonderful animal dream facts
to discover: birds dream of songs, for example, and cows

sleep standing up but need to lie down to dream, and dolphins let only half of their brain sleep at a time.

Although we think our dreams only last a few seconds, current research suggests we dream in real time. And all of us, male and female, become fully sexually stimulated in REM sleep, which seems rather ironic since we're paralysed and cannot act on those biological impulses. Nor does REM sleep diminish with age. No one has yet come up with the definitive reason for this REM phenomenon, but it may have something to do with the role our dreams play in balancing our internal gender issues, and also sex acts are generally stimulated by desire, which is one of the primary motivational factors in our dreams.

Curiously, if the part of the brain that regulates the physiological condition of REM is removed, we still dream, yet if the part of the brain to do with desire and motivation is removed, we do not dream. There's a lot of scientific research that claims that dreaming is a purely physiological processing system, but for me, this fact alone would argue against that. If dreams were solely biological in purpose, I can't see a reason why we would stop dreaming if we lost our desire and motivation, yet we do. We need desire and motivation to dream.

Also, during the REM cycle the chemicals that relate to the logical, rational aspects of our brain are all switched off and all our emotive, creative, solution-seeking chemicals are switched on and powered up. It is, without doubt, an incredibly creative period. This is why I encourage you to use dreams actively. We're wasting a massive creative resource by not tapping into this chemical opportunity.

Hormones

Research has shown that female hormonal cycles can affect women's dreams. Women tend to get more emotional or nightmarish dreams just before a period. They can even have violent blood-and-guts-type dreams and awaken to find their period has started.

There's also a lot of anecdotal evidence that women going into their menopausal years get dreams of giving birth. I've had several such dreams reported to me.

One of my students, a post-menopausal lady, reported more prophetic dreams during the hormonal rollercoaster of her menopause. Here's one such dream she had:

My daughter was ill in 2000. At the beginning of 2001 I dreamed that I was walking by myself through a lunar landscape with craters. I was walking very slowly and carefully so as not to fall into any of the craters.

As I was walking, my car came past me with my husband driving and my daughter in the passenger seat. They went past me and into a crater. I said to myself, 'My husband is getting killed as well.'

I went on walking, still being very careful to avoid the craters, and I had a white scarf in my hand. I looked down and saw a lama sitting next to a pool of water. The scarf fell from my hand and landed on the water and just floated there. I called out to the lama, 'Can you help me?'

'Yes,' he said. 'What can I do?'

'You can pass me the scarf,' I said, and he did. He handed it up to me and I continued walking.

Then there was a whole row of shelves and on the top shelf there was a bassinet with a beautiful baby boy in it and he sat up and gave me a big smile.

When I woke, I knew my husband was going to collapse, which he did two weeks later. I saw very clearly that's what would happen, as both he and my daughter had gone into the crater... My daughter was already ill, but I knew from the baby and the lama that somehow it would be all right. My daughter has since recovered, although my husband is still not well.

Since my menopause I have had far more precognitive dreams of this nature.

Hypnos

There are two final sleep stages that will prove to be valuable assistants in our creative process and are an essential part of our dreaming repertoire.

The two states have many characteristics in common. They're not fully understood, though anecdotal evidence suggests they're responsible for many strange sleep phenomena and if we understand their basic nature we can put them to excellent use.

The first is the hypnagogic state. This is effectively the process of falling asleep. In this state we are neither awake nor asleep, but suspended temporarily in between. Sometimes we have a very real sense of falling at the onset of sleep and can awaken with a jump.

It's an odd transition going from waking to sleeping and it doesn't happen immediately. People have reported hallucinations, ghostly sightings, strange visions, bizarre thoughts and many other phenomena during this phase of sleep. Often we don't remember anything from this state, as we're soon deeply asleep. If we are disturbed during this period, though, we can often recall vivid visions. These are in-between dreams, half-waking visions and half-real dreams. They tend to be short and exhibit fewer of the bizarre dream phenomena that can happen later in full REM sleep.

From Harvard scientists' experiments with brain-damaged patients it has emerged that hypnagogic dreams are possible even when suffering from severe amnesia, proving we don't need conscious memory to have these kinds of dreams. This means they tap into our internal databanks, and we can use this idea to tap into ours through this dreaming gate, which we'll learn to do in Chapter Eleven.

The second state is the hypnopompic stage. This is the transition out of sleep into wakefulness. A reasonably common phenomenon of this stage is being slightly out of synch with the body's sleep paralysis system. This is still switched on, but the mind has woken up. The result is a sense of suffocation. It can feel as though something is pinning you to the bed. This is often accompanied by strange hallucinations and it has been hypothesized that this is perhaps the true cause of many ghost sightings, as there are numerous reported cases of seeing presences in the room, feeling shadowy figures pressing down, hearing manic laughter, etc., in this state. It can be a terrifying experience, as you're lucid but can't move a muscle. You're back in that twilight zone again, neither awake nor asleep but somewhere, momentarily suspended, betwixt those worlds.

As there is a degree of lucidity present in the hypnopompic state, if you ever find yourself experiencing this, having read about it, you'll now remember what it is and be able to relax, knowing it will quickly pass. It's been proven that stress creates more likelihood of this occurring, so the more we can relax in the moment, the more quickly it will be over. If we try to fight it, on the other hand, our physiology in that state reacts and makes it a far more traumatic experience.

The sleep paralysis mechanism is also involved in other dream experiences. When we hit out in our dreams or wake up screaming, we've experienced such an intense dream that it's broken through the paralysis and we've woken up. Or it may be that we're at the end of a REM cycle and the paralysis switch has been thrown just that little bit early. Perhaps something in our environment disturbed our sleep or our alarm clock went off. So, if we were in the middle of a fist fight in our dream, we may hit someone sleeping peacefully next to us!

REM Shifts

The amount of time we spend in REM sleep changes as we develop. Newborn babies spend more than 70 per cent of their sleeping time in it. Even foetuses dream. But by the time we're six months old, the time spent in REM sleep has dropped considerably, to barely more than that spent by the average adult. This is still far more than the REM sleep of an elderly person who, by contrast, may only spend a fraction of their sleeping cycle in that stage.

It would appear babies need this extra dreamtime to assimilate the data assault they're experiencing. Suddenly they're forcefully expelled from their cosy womb into a world of enormous beings and information overload. One of the hypothesized functions of dreaming is to file and process our experiences, and babies need to process the overwhelming array of information they're bombarded with in order to speed their rate of growth and development. An elderly person, on the other hand, has fewer new opportunities and new adventures and less need to process new information. They've built up their knowledge and experience and expect the world to behave in a certain way. That's not to say that they stop dreaming; they still have significant dreams, but they tend to be less frequent.

Of course, babies and children do not remember every one of their many dreams. Many of them just involve the learning and processing part of the brain that allows them to adapt, grow and develop. However, evidence from my dream groups does suggest that there may be a direct correlation between children's nightmares and future events in their lives, as this example from the singer and pianist Ian Shaw highlights:

As a child I had a recurring dream. I was sliding down a helter skelter which was brightly coloured and placed on a very choppy sea. The winds were howling and the helter skelter was swaying from side to side as I sat there, clutching my little hessian mat and never ever reaching the bottom – which would, of course, have plunged me into the stormy sea below. Inevitably, as I felt I was about to plunge into the said water, I would wake up screaming.

This sporadic nightmare continued into my university days before stopping suddenly.

Ten years ago, I took my young niece and nephew to the annual funfair in London's Leicester Square.

'Ian, Ian, the helter skelter!'

'OK, kids! Off we go!'

We climbed the tall red and yellow contraption and I watched as my little charges whizzed down the chute, screaming with joy. I hauled my 15 stone onto the tiny mat and sat at the top of the slide. A tiny seed of doubt had sown itself into my mind, but there was no backing down now. Besides, there were small people behind me waiting their turn.

I let myself loose down the chute and sped around the helter skelter, shooting off the bottom with the velocity of a small bull shot out of a cannon. I landed some ten metres from the bottom of the slide and felt a sharp pain at my rear end.

Many specialists later, I was told that my coccyx was permanently damaged by a hairline crack.

My 'tail' is never going to be mended.

Dreams and Chinese Medicine

Finally, a word about dreams and Chinese medicine. According to this discipline, there are five spirits in the body that govern wellness and illness. Two of these have a relationship to dreams. There's Shen, which relates to our true spirit. It governs the heart and in Chinese medicine it's the heart that houses the soul. Dreams that are powerful and feel right to us come from our heart. However, there's another energy, called Hun, which is generated in the liver. If you're experiencing consistently disturbed sleep, many crazy dreams that are proving exhausting, and tend to wake around 4 a.m., then your liver energy may be out of balance. The Hun energy pulls on the heart, in effect pulling your spirit from the centre of your heart.

A 45-year-old mother from my dream circles illustrates how this imbalance can manifest. She tragically lost her 26-year-old daughter, her only child, to cancer. She was a single, self-employed, socially isolated mum with minimal family support. Her dreams began shortly after the death of her daughter. Before then she'd had reasonable numbers of dreams but nothing out of the ordinary; now she was experiencing up to five or six vivid dreams a night. She was able to remember these in detail upon waking and record them in reams.

She joined my dream circle 13 months after the death. During that time the dreams had continued to grow in intensity and she was becoming more and more exhausted until eventually I suggested she stop recording her dreams for a while and see an acupuncturist who could assist her in releasing her grief and balancing her liver energy. However, she was able to release some of her repressed grief though the dream group. At the start, the loss of her daughter had left her feeling so helpless that her dreaming mind consistently took her back to the last time she'd experienced that loss of power, which had been as a child, and they took place in her old house from childhood:

In a lot of my dreams my mum is not in them but present. I'm always aware of her being there or being at her house and never seeing her. A lot of my dreams will happen outside her house in the back garden. Or maybe not outside the house but around the house. They're never nice dreams.

Some months later, progress was being made. Transport in dreams is always about our journey in life, and houses are about aspects of our psyche. The woman described her most recent sequence of dreams:

I was on many buses and many tubes. The mobile phone came up several times. House rebuilding, house renovating and recycling all recurred. The number six came up quite a few times and the number three came up a few times. My daughter was always alive in the dreams and was dying in six months' time. That just kept coming up. I had to prepare everything because I knew she was going to die in six months' time.

*Then I dreamed it was her funeral and I was really happy.
I was so, so happy because all my friends from work were
coming to see me. I was really happy. But my daughter wasn't
anywhere around. It was as if it wasn't her funeral, but I knew
it was her funeral because my friends from work were coming
to my house for it and I was really happy.*

This dreamer is being asked to begin to let the grieving go.
It's coming to a conclusion, she's not having to hold on to it
in the same way as before. There's also a strong message to
connect to others and not become isolated – this is the route to
her renewed happiness.

By the time you've worked through this book your dreams
will have revealed their power to you too. But first it's time
for the dream gym and your pre-dreaming assessment.

CHAPTER TWO

To Sleep Is to Dream

Bedroom Design for Healthy Sleep and Dreams

'We fear death, yet we long for slumber and beautiful dreams.'
Kahlil Gibran

Becoming a champion dreamer requires preparation. For our dreams to come true we need to set up optimum conditions for success. We wouldn't expect to win a race without having spent time training.

To hear the whispers of our dreaming selves the starting point is a good night's sleep. Research tells us highly creative people sleep more. Einstein was a champion sleeper, regularly clocking up 10 hours a night – even more if he was involved in a particularly juicy project.

In ancient times, dream temples and healing sanctuaries were deemed an important part of everyday life. We're going to replicate the energy of these healing environments by creating a modern dream temple. Let your bedroom become what it should be – a sanctuary that nourishes and restores your body and feeds your mind and spirit, a place where genius dreams are guaranteed!

We all have an innate understanding of how our environment affects us. We know that we immediately get a good feeling when we enter some houses and a bad feeling when we enter others. We know instinctively if an argument has taken place there. Our language supports our understanding; we may say, 'You could cut the atmosphere with a knife.' We don't consciously think about this, and if we do, we probably call it 'good or bad vibes'. The ancient Chinese, however, had a whole area of study devoted to this subject, known as *feng shui*.

What is *Feng Shui*?

Feng shui is a system for creating balance and harmony in our life through the manipulation of the flow of energy around our home. Originally it was only the Chinese emperors who had access to this knowledge, and they used it to maintain their wealth and power. Gradually, however, the wisdom was disseminated throughout the general populace. It remains practical and relevant today.

We can use the principles of *feng shui* to help us design a bedroom conducive to restful sleep and quality dreams – a modern-day version of the dream temples of old. We want a bedroom that oozes dreamlike sensuality and embraces us in an enveloping hug when we walk into it.

It works based on what quantum physics teaches us about everything in the universe being connected and made of energy. Therefore, everything in our homes has a corresponding impact on our life, either good or bad, because we are energetically connected to it. It is relatively easy to see how colour in a room, natural light, the style of furniture, type of art, ornaments, presence of living plants, etc., can affect our experience of it and determine whether or not we feel comfortable there. What perhaps is more difficult for us to grasp immediately is the notion that invisible energy flows around us all the time and that anything that affects that flow will also affect our life.

To get an idea of this and connect to a new understanding of your living space, do the following exercise, which takes you on a journey through your home.

General Advice for Journeying

Please do not attempt any of the journeys whilst driving or operating any kind of machinery. They're designed to put you in a light self-hypnotic trance. If you've never experienced anything like this before, it is perfectly safe and is a feeling akin to deep relaxation or a meditative state. The biggest obstacle to doing any of this work is our own resistance. We need to be able to give ourselves permission to journey.

All the journeys in this book are perfectly safe for you to do on your own. You might like to record them on tape and play them back or get a friend to read them to you. You will get the best results if you find a comfortable place to sit or lie down and completely relax, somewhere where you will be undisturbed for 15 or 20 minutes.

A DREAM JOURNEY FOR CONNECTING TO YOUR HOME

Read through the following text a couple of times to familiarize yourself with it. Then allow your intuition to guide you on this journey. There's no need to be physically at home in order to do it. If you're away, you can still do it. Sometimes you get a more powerful experience if you have some physical distance between you and your home.

Have a notebook or journal with you and some coloured pens or pencils.

Get relaxed and allow yourself to become empty and receptive by focusing on your natural breathing for a few minutes. Just observe your breath – do not try to change it in any way.

Feel the gentle gravitational pull of the Earth below you gently pulling you into it. It's very comforting to feel how we are magnetically attached to the planet.

Close your eyes and imagine yourself walking along the street to your home. See yourself approaching the front door of your home. Look around. What do you feel? What do you hear? What do you see? What gets your attention as you walk towards your house?

Just observe rather than judge what happens. There is no right and wrong, there just is.

Open your front door and walk into your hallway, closing the door behind you. Pause for a moment. How does it feel to be home? What emotions or feelings are present as you stand in your hallway?

Continue on your journey through your home. There's only your own path to follow, but make sure you visit each area. Where do you automatically want to head for once inside? What's there? Who's there? What do you feel, hear, see and notice, maybe even smell?

Wander slowly around the inside of your home, visiting each room, feeling what you feel, hearing what you hear, seeing what you see and noticing what you notice.

Observe your body language as you move from room to room. Do you hesitate anywhere? Is there a room you quickly move on from? Is there an area where you do not want to linger?

Pay particular attention when you get to your bedroom. Pause. Sit on the bed. Tune in to how you feel here. If you could name the energy you feel, what would it be?

Look around, lie down. What do you see? What do you hear? What do you notice?

What repeats? What stands out? What is exaggerated?

When you have finished, walk to the front door and leave, thanking your home for the insights and secrets it has offered up to you.

Slowly bring your awareness back into your body, stretch a few times and wriggle your toes and fingers.

Record in your notebook or journal anything that stood out in your mind and anything else that was of meaning to you. Perhaps there was a colour that sprang to mind when you entered a room, or an idea for decoration. Also consider the answers to the following questions:

✱ What is the most important room in my home for me?

✱ Where is the heart of my home?

✱ Where do I spend most time in my home?

✱ Where do I feel safest in my home?

By doing this exercise you'll have discovered that a home is remarkably chatty for a supposedly inanimate object! If you follow the advice your home gives to you in this exercise, you will be delighted with the changes both inside and out.

Trained in *feng shui*, when I'm encouraging dreams I focus on people's bedrooms. So many clients complain about poor sleep or lack of sleep that I have made the bedroom my specialist subject. Sleep is vital for our physical and mental well-being. We need deep, restorative rest in order to keep our immune system healthy and repair the body's worn-out cells. In addition, we need time for dreams to process our mental data, reflect our truth to us and stimulate our creativity.

So take a look at your bedroom. What was the quality of energy you felt there when you did the house meditation? Did it feel balanced, calm, restful, a true temple to dreams? Great, leave it that way. If it didn't, then use what you felt as a guideline for making changes. Energetic shifts can be created with lighting, colour, furniture, plants, textures, furnishings, artwork, etc.

Our homes are an external representation of who we are. If we change something in our home we will experience a corresponding shift in our life. The same principle applies to dreams. How we live in the world will make a difference to the dreams we experience and how we dream will make a difference to how we live.

Clutter Holds Back your Dreams

Feng shui is all about creating balance in an environment. If a place feels too hot, we need to cool it down. If it's too sharp, we need to soften it up. If it moves too fast, we need to slow it down. If it's too slow, we need to speed it up. So let's apply that to our bedroom.

To experience powerful dreams we need to allow a good healthy flow of energy through our bedroom. The ideal bedroom would have just a bed in it. Obviously that's not practical for modern living, where our idealism gets squashed by too much stuff and too little space. But it's a useful guideline to encourage us to minimize the number of distractions surrounding us whilst we sleep.

Let's consider the important difference between storage and clutter. Storage is neat, tidy, clean and accessible. Items classified as storage can be defined as being valuable, useful or treasured, ideally all three. Anything you don't use, love or need is clutter.

If we're honest, many bedrooms (and homes generally) are overflowing with clutter desperately masquerading as something useful. But clutter holds you back in life. It impedes the smooth flow of energy around your space, and having too much becomes a drain on your energy, stopping your progress. To inspire you to get those bin bags out, think of it this way: you're attached energetically to absolutely everything you own. If you love it, that energy feels light and nourishing; if it's clutter, it's like dragging around a ball and chain. Ask yourself: 'How many balls and chains am I carrying around?'

Although your whole house would probably benefit from a visit from the clutter police, I'm going to stick specifically to bedroom clutter here. This includes everything from unwanted gifts and unfinished jobs that gnaw away at you to half-read magazines and piles of books that you've been meaning to get round to. And what about your clothes? Make sure they are within wardrobes, not scattered all over the floor. Clear out overfilled wardrobes and give away clothes that look good on another you. All these things drag you down and reduce your ability to sleep peacefully.

TOP TIP

The quickest way to lose weight is to only have clothes in your wardrobe that fit the size you are right now. By fully accepting who you are in this moment, you will find the excess weight magically begins to disappear.

If you're reading this at home, look around your bedroom now and identify where your energy-draining clutter is.

Places to look:

* on top of the wardrobe
* inside the wardrobe
* under the bed
* all drawers
* bedside cabinets
* shelf units
* window ledges.

Remember we're creating a sanctuary here, so the clutter goes. All those excess things are a burden and they're getting in the way of your mind-blowing dreams! Besides which, clutter in our bedrooms can specifically impact on our health, especially the stuff under our beds. We spend one third of our day in direct contact with where we sleep. Ideally, keep the space under the bed free or use it to store clean towels and bed linen only.

As well as benefiting your well-being and encouraging your dreams, clearing clutter in your bedroom will support your recovery from an illness.

TOP TIP

If you are ill, put a bowl of dry natural rock salt by your bed at night. This absorbs the toxins you breathe out whilst ill and supports a faster recovery. Change the salt daily and throw the old salt away.

If possible, keep the dirty laundry basket somewhere other than your bedroom, perhaps in the bathroom, the hallway or a dressing room (if you have one). There should be no TV in the bedroom either, and no work. If you have to work in the bedroom then buy a screen and use it to cover up your work once you have finished for the day. If the last thing you see before sleep is a pile of unfinished jobs and a long 'to do list', it is distracting and unhelpful. More than that, it will adversely affect the content of your dreams. This is about creating a bedroom that is a contemporary temple for sleep and dreaming. We're creating a sacred space for honouring our life and our dreams.

Location, Location, Location

The physical location of bedrooms is important. They are best sited towards the back of the house where it tends to be quieter away from busy main roads. Positioned here, we will naturally sleep more deeply. We feel vulnerable with a bedroom near the front door. If the bedroom is outside the home, perhaps in an extension, our energy will be outside the house and we will find ourselves spending more time away from home. If our bedroom is over a garage, it creates an unstable footing and we'll be prone to restless, unsatisfying sleep.

Where the bed is positioned in the room is one of the main factors that can affect the energy and quality of sleep. Ideally, your feet will not directly face the open door of the bedroom. You'll feel uncomfortable in this position because your energy system is open – the energy from the soles of your feet can shoot out through the door. This prevents you from being cocooned in a safe boundary whilst asleep. If you cannot change the bed position, you can benefit from a solid barrier at the foot of the bed, either a piece of furniture such as a chest of drawers or a footboard on the bed itself.

Avoid putting the bed behind the door if the door opens towards the bed, as you want to be able to see who is coming in. If you have your bed with the head against a window you will tend to feel a subtle sense of vulnerability. In this case, if you cannot change the position of the bed, ensure it has a good solid headboard. For optimum support, ideally all beds should have headboards and these should be made of wood, leather or natural fabrics and be solid rather than slatted.

Keep the area behind the bedroom door clear so the door can open freely.

The ideal bed position has a solid wall behind with a clear view of the door. This is known as the 'power position'. Figure 1 illustrates the power position alternatives that are available for you to sleep in.

Bedroom Irritants

Check your bedroom for sharp corners which could be pointing at your bed, as these accelerate the flow of energy

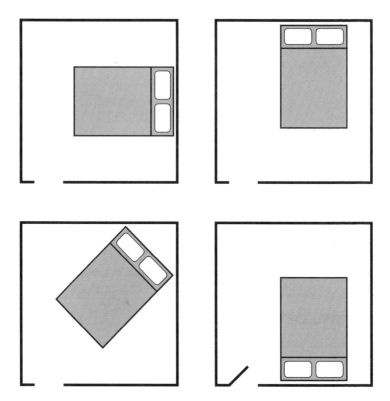

FIG 1. Ideal bed positions

and the force of this energy rushing towards you can have a negative impact. Be aware of scale. A wardrobe at the other end of the bedroom would not necessarily be seen as threatening, but if it's close to the bed or you have other square corners from large bedside tables or sideboards, you would do well to see whether you can change the layout. My clients can testify to the long-term effect of such placements, which have resulted in physical health issues where the projected energy line crosses their bodies. You can cure the problem easily by draping the sharp corners in trailing plants such as ivy or using cloth covers to soften the edges.

Many old homes have beams above the bed. Sleeping underneath a beam is best avoided, as it creates a downward energetic pressure whilst you sleep. To cure this, move your bed to a new position under an even ceiling. If this is impossible, then you can minimize the effect of the beam by painting it the same colour as the ceiling, enabling it to blend in. Alternatively, you can put up a muslin or mosquito-net type of covering above the bed to create a safe sleeping canopy in the way they used to do with four-poster beds. Or you can place up-lighters directly under the beams to counteract the downward energy.

To encourage healthy sleep I recommend using natural bedding. Cotton, silk, linen, hemp – any natural fabrics are great for your bed. Man-made fibres tend to create static electricity, which can interfere with your sleeping and hence your dreaming processes.

'Who's Been Sleeping in my Bed?'

Another thing that has a significant impact on how a space feels is the issue of who lived there before you or what, in *feng shui* terms, is called 'predecessor *chi*'. When a space is used for a purpose, the energy moving around inside tends to leave an imprint or memory and over time this invisible pattern builds up in intensity. For example, houses inhabited by happy families with children tend to attract couples who want a family. Similarly, homes sold by a divorced couple tend to attract a long line of divorces as history repeats itself. The psychic residue of the events that have taken place there causes this. Houses can be cleared of these unhelpful blueprints, creating a blank canvas for something new to take place. Simple techniques for safely clearing your own space are listed at the end of this chapter.

With regard to your bedroom, it is worth giving some thought to who last slept in your bed besides you. Was it a healthy relationship? Is it ongoing? Did it end painfully? The psychic residue of that person will be in the fabric of the bed itself. If it's healthy and ongoing, great, leave well alone. If it's over but still haunting you, then clear your bed to reclaim your sleep and your dreams. It's simple to do. Treat yourself to some new bed linen as a minimum. If a lot of angst has taken place, for example you've been through a painful divorce and are still sleeping in the marital bed, seriously consider getting a new bed, or at the very least a new mattress. If it is less serious than that, take a baseball bat or rolling pin and simply beat the old negative energies out of the mattress. Turn the mattress over and give everything a good shake. This can be therapeutic on many levels, depending on the nature of that old relationship!

QUICK WAYS TO CLEAR AND ENERGIZE YOUR BEDROOM

* Clap loudly in all the corners.

* Ring a bell around the room clockwise.

* Burn some incense – Nitraj is the best brand for clearing spaces. (*See Resources at the back of the book for details.*)

* Play some loud music with plenty of bass (preferably not if the neighbours are home!)

* Open all the doors and windows for five minutes and get some fresh air circulating.

'Mirror, Mirror on the Wall...'

Mirrors in the bedroom have a massive impact on the quality of our sleep, especially if we can see ourselves in them whilst in bed. The object of a mirror is to magnify a space, to make it look larger, and therefore it is expanding the energy in a room. When we sleep, our body needs to be calm and settled. Our energy needs to be directed internally to focus on any necessary repair work, to dream and to seek solutions to our problems. Mirrors work against this natural process.

Accordingly, remove any mirrors that you can, or cover them over with a scarf at night. If you have mirrored wardrobes, you can cover the doors in frosting. One company even custom designs the doors from your personal photographs, enabling you to wake up to your own sultry beach scene or snowy mountain top. (*See Resources.*)

Décor

Décor in the bedroom ideally veers towards subtle and sensual rather than bold and brash. In our bedrooms it is important to create a calming, relaxing flow of energy to promote restorative sleep and healthy dreams. This means smooth patterns without abrupt changes from one design to another, and a subdued colour scheme.

Look around at the patterns and colours in your bedroom:

* Are the colours too vibrant and stark?
* Do the patterns clash?
* Is there too much abrupt change between the colours?
* Are there too many different patterns?
* Are the patterns themselves awkward?

Jules Standish, colour and style consultant, tells us:

The colours we choose for our bedrooms strongly affect us because when we are asleep we absorb energy more quickly. The body and mind recharge themselves whilst we sleep and if the room is decorated with a mixture of bright colours, particularly yellow and red, then our nervous system will continue to be stimulated and we won't wake up feeling relaxed. Cool colours like blue will calm the activity of our brain, which will affect the quality and quantity of our dreams, encouraging peaceful and deep sleep. Blue can be mixed with the balancing hues of green to make turquoise, which is very relaxing and goes particularly well with the loving warmer shades of pink. Violet is a wonderful colour for helping to stimulate dreams of spirituality, as it is connected to the third eye. This colour in a bedroom inspires us to listen to our body and what it needs to take us through a particularly dramatic emotional period.

You may find simply engaging in the process of creating a sanctuary provokes your dreaming mind to offer some helpful hints in terms of colour, décor, etc. For the best results, do act on these suggestions of your dreaming attention if they appear.

Invisible Nasties

Research shows that pollution inside our homes can be ten times greater than outside. This comes in all sorts of hidden forms, from air fresheners to household cleaners, toxic paint fumes, outgassing from new synthetic carpets, electromagnetic frequencies (EMFs) and microwave radiation.

Some people are far more sensitive to these toxic frequencies than others in exactly the same way that some people suffer food allergies and others don't. Location, genetics, upbringing, habits and income all play a part in our overall well-being and susceptibility to these nasties.

The good news is there are always things we can do to improve our environment. We also have the power of resilience and the ability to self-heal. This section will empower you with the knowledge and skills to cure your bedroom, and home in general, of modern toxicity and health hazards. If you suffer from headaches, irritability, ME, insomnia or other sleep disturbances, then it is particularly worth exploring the advice given here.

EMFs

An EMF, electromagnetic field, is a field of energy created by an electrically charged object. You can't see, feel or hear electromagnetic fields, apart from visible light, which is a part of the electromagnetic spectrum. We have evolved with the natural levels of EMFs produced by both the sun and world around us. However, the Earth's magnetic fields are static fields, unlike man-made alternating current (AC), which has no natural counterpart. Microwave frequency, too, is a relatively new phenomenon: 100 years ago the background radiation was millions of times lower than it is now. It has only been since the recent mobile phone boom that modern, digitally pulsed signals have become ubiquitous in the Western world.

Research has shown that exposure to high EMFs, especially near the head, can interfere with the efficiency of the pineal gland, which releases melatonin and serotonin. In those who are sensitive, this can lead to sleep disturbances and depression. With long-term exposure these discordant frequencies also lower our immune system.

Sources of EMFs in the bedroom include electric blankets, clock radios, TVs, music systems and hairdryers. The problem is exacerbated if you use synthetic bed linen and have a metal bed, as this increases the conductive ability of the electric currents.

TOP TIP

Use this ancient shamanic practice to get your daily dose of beneficial Earth energies.

Stand with your left palm facing the ground and your right hand resting by your side (regardless of whether you are right or left-handed). Imagine the energy of the Earth soaking into you through your left palm, the soles of your feet and your perineum, just like a sponge soaking up water.

Do for five minutes daily or when you feel you need it.

Digital cordless phones, mobile phones and wi-fi all give off microwave emissions. Increasingly research suggests links to loss of memory, headaches, premature ageing and tumours from this type of radiation.

Outgassing from poisons, including formaldehyde in new furniture, carpets and some paints, combined with sealed double glazing, leads to new homes becoming toxic incubators. In such houses we can wake up with headaches, nausea, flu-like symptoms, allergies, dermatitis and a general feeling of malaise.

TOP TIP

Always sleep in a well-ventilated room. If you cannot sleep with a window open, air the room thoroughly before going to bed.

For those of you who watch TV in bed or, worse still, fall asleep with it on, the imperceptible flickering of the screen creates oscillations that cause abnormal responses in the brain, bringing about headaches, eyestrain and fatigue. Pause for a moment to think what it does to your dreams too. When we lose consciousness, the hearing is the last sense to go. Sleep lab research has indicated that alarms, doorbells and other external sounds become part of our dreams. Think what those late-night TV and radio shows are doing to your dreams. This is indiscriminate self-hypnosis! At least ensure that what you listen to as you drift off is what you want to be programming your mind with!

Geopathic Stress

Lastly, there is what is known as geo(Earth)pathic(disease) stress (GS). This occurs when the natural electromagnetic field of the Earth becomes distorted. It's the term used for areas of the Earth that are stressed out and sick. If we spend a long time sleeping or sitting on lines of GS we too can become stressed out and sick if we are sensitive to these energies. This may be entirely new information to you, but GS has been extensively researched and documented over the years (*see Resources for more information*).

Common signs of GS include chronic clutter, light bulbs blowing frequently, electrical items malfunctioning more often than is considered normal, a musty, damp smell, a general feeling of unease or discomfort, plagues of ants or wasps, ivy, nettles, poor plant growth and twisted trees.

Certain animals are either repelled or attracted by these energies. Cats love them and dogs avoid them. We need to use common sense, though; the cat sleeping on the end of our bed does not guarantee we have GS – it may just be the cat's favourite place to be! Babies will tend to sleep away from GS, though, and a good indication that there's a problem is if you regularly find your baby curled up in an odd cot corner. They actually look as though they are trying to get away from something. In terms of our bedrooms, the main thing we need to know with GS is that we're not sleeping on it.

TOP TIP

To check for GS in your bedroom, take an old wire coat hanger. Untwist the hanger part and break it in two or use wire cutters to cut it. You should have two similar-sized halves that you can bend into two 90-degree angled dowsing rods.

Walk slowly from one side of your room to the other and see if the rods react. Now walk slowly the other way and see if they react.

If they cross over or react wildly, see where this line is in relation to your bed. If it crosses it, move your bed to a position free of any crossing lines.

This works because we have a natural affinity with the healthy EMF of the Earth and anything discordant will affect our energy field and react via the dowsing rods. (*To buy professional dowsing rods, see Resources.*)

If the above seems too difficult and you're concerned about the possibility of GS, consider employing a professional dowser (*again, see Resources*).

If you cannot move your bed, there are alternative solutions for GS, including a number of plug-in devices such as the Raditech and the Helios (*see Resources*). In my experience the Helios is the more effective product. However, the most effective long-term cure is Earth acupuncture, which works in exactly the same way as traditional acupuncture except you treat the meridians of the Earth with large wooden needles, rather than the body with small metal needles (*see Resources*).

What Can We Do to Protect Ourselves?

We cannot avoid the onslaught of the modern world. Even if we resist wi-fi and the digital age, if our neighbour installs it we'll be affected anyway. If we live in an urban area, then every time we step outside we are being bombarded with these frequencies. So what can we do to protect ourselves?

Actually quite a bit. Remember the big issue with all of these frequencies is that they are in opposition to our naturally produced EMFs. It is not that they actually cause physical illness (well, it's not yet definitely proven anyway), but they subtly stress our system, which over time leads to a lowering of the immune system, which can then lead to more serious conditions. So the key is to keep your immune system as healthy as possible. We already know what can help with this: a good diet, plenty of water, exercise, etc. We also need good sleep, as our immune system is repaired and strengthened during the night. Ensure your bedroom is as supportive as possible by following this action plan:

HEALTHY BEDROOM ACTION PLAN

* Keep your bedroom as electrically silent as possible. Unplug all items near the bed before sleep or, for the ultimate in peaceful sleep, get your electrician to install a power demand switch for the bedroom circuit. This will enable you to turn off the electricity supply to your bedroom at night. (You'll need a torch nearby as the lights won't work.)

* Use a battery or wind-up alarm clock, *never* your mobile phone. Keep digital handsets and especially base stations a long way from the bedroom. These emit powerful radio signals that can interfere with our healthy electromagnetic energy. You might like to invest in Orchard dect low-radiation phones, which are a healthier alternative (*see Resources for details*), or use an old-fashioned plug-in phone.

* Place peace lilies and/or spider plants in rooms with electrical equipment, PCs, etc. These plants are particularly efficient at removing EMFs from the atmosphere.

* Plug in an ionizer in rooms with electrical equipment to release negative ions into the atmosphere to counteract all the positive ions being belched out by the equipment.

* Cheaper than the above – use a *damp*, not wet, cloth to wipe over your computer screen and keyboard each morning before use. It adds negative ions to the atmosphere.

* Place a bowl of sea salt in the office. (Remember to throw it away after a few days and replace it with a new batch.) Salt is great at absorbing environmental pollutants. Please don't use the salt for any culinary purpose afterwards, as it will spoil your food.

✳ Place unpolished clear quartz crystals on fuse boxes and electricity meters and near your computer. These soak up the pollutants. Be aware they do get 'full', though, and will need cleansing regularly by rinsing under the tap in clean running water or burying in the garden for 24 hours.

✳ Use stick-on protective phone shields for your walkabout phones, mobiles and PCs. There are many to choose from; the ones I recommend and have tested are the quartz phoneshields (see Resources).

✳ Plug in a Helios device (also great for harmonizing geopathic stress). It's the cheapest, smallest and in my experience the best on the market of these devices. Others include the Geomack or Raditech (see Resources).

Encouraging Deep Sleep and Meaningful Dreams

We've become out of tune with the natural cycles and rhythms of nature. The best cellular healing time for the body is between 11 p.m. and 3 a.m. Get to sleep before 11 p.m. for optimum health.

If you have trouble sleeping, even with the changes you've made to your bedroom, ensure you're not too hot. Our body temperature needs to be cooling down in order to induce sleep, hence why we find it hard to sleep on hot summer nights. Avoid hot baths less than two hours before bedtime.

You might like to use a herb pillow stuffed with lavender and rosemary to help you drift off. Alternatively, place aromatherapy rings on the light bulbs of your bedside lamps and add a few drops of lavender oil to them. These allow you to benefit from the oils without the need for potentially dangerous candles.

If you are suffering from nightmares, there is evidence to suggest some of them are a way of relieving stress in the body, so to encourage more pleasurable dreams, do some meditation or relaxation exercises on retiring that allow the body to relax. There are hundreds to choose from these days, or you could learn the autogenic technique, an excellent process for inducing deep relaxation (*see Resources*).

The following is a relaxation exercise I find very beneficial:

RELEASING TENSION IN THE BODY

✻ Get comfortable in bed and then begin to scan your physical body, starting with your toes.

✻ Scrunch up your toes really tight, hold for a count of three, then let go and allow yourself to follow the letting-go feeling. Imagine yourself smiling into your toes and sinking into that feeling.

✻ Continue the same process with each part of your body.

I've never managed to finish the entire body yet, as I'm always asleep before that happens!

Another way of encouraging sleep is to buy a beautiful piece of amethyst crystal for your bedside cabinet (*see Resources*). Amethyst is excellent for reducing the incidence of nightmares, whilst also helping with insomnia.

Or you could indulge in what's known as a dream catcher. In ancient times Native Americans used to weave dream catchers to catch all the bad dreams and only let the good ones in. With the light of a new dawn all the bad dreams would be released back to whence they'd come and only the positive ones kept.

FENG SHUI CHECKLIST FOR CREATING A PERSONAL DREAM SANCTUARY

* Bedrooms should be a sanctuary, ideally just a bed.

* Clear your clutter – a cluttered bedroom leads to a cluttered mind!

* No overhanging wardrobes or heavy shelves above the bed – it makes you feel vulnerable and overwhelmed.

* Don't place the bed opposite the door or under a window, as it leads to feelings of insecurity.

* Get a good solid headboard to make you feel secure and supported, preferably one made of wood or natural fabric.

* Let fresh air in at night.

* Avoid sleeping under sloping ceilings and beams if possible – it can make you feel depressed and overburdened.

* Mirrors activate and energize you, so avoid sleeping where you can see yourself reflected in one.

* Avoid sharp corners from bedroom furniture 'attacking' you. You can often use a cloth or a trailing plant to cover the corners.

* Keep the colour mostly neutral, with a splash of boldness to activate passion. Too much red will cause sleepless nights.

* Have something inspiring to wake up to – a picture with depth of field, for example a pathway through a forest or a horizon. (*See Resources*.)

* Use natural-fibre bed linen, ideally organic cotton, which allows skin to breathe.

Space Clearing

We've got our bedrooms looking fabulous; now it's time
to lavish some attention on the atmosphere of our dream
sanctuary.

Space clearing and purifying the energy of living spaces
are practices that have been employed by indigenous cultures
since time immemorial. It is the original meaning behind the
Western concept of house-warming parties. Such events clear
out the psychic residue of the previous inhabitants and allow
the space to be effused with our friends' and family's energy.
For me, this process is as essential as physically cleaning and
tidying our space. We wouldn't want to sleep in somebody
else's dirty sheets, so why would we want to live in their old
energy field?

I recommend a major space clearing at least once a year
or following any kind of big change in your life – a new job,
being made redundant, the break-up of a relationship, a major
illness, moving house, etc. This enables the release of the
emotional and mental stress that accumulates in our space and
allows us to enjoy a fresh start.

If this is the first time you've heard of such a process or
you are aware that your home has a history of trauma, then I
would recommend you employ an expert such as myself to
space clear your home for you. Otherwise, the process given
here is perfectly safe to do on your own bedroom or home and
creates a wonderful intention for your adventure in dreaming.
I do not recommend you cleanse other people's spaces unless
you have been properly trained.

MINI-HOME SPACE CLEAR

Our home as well as our body can stagnate over time. Give yours an energetic detox and revive your health, wealth and happiness by following this simple process. This clearing raises the energetic vibration of your home to allow it to become more in tune with what you wish to manifest in your life. With this technique we change the resonance of a space by working with sound and the smoke of sacred herbs.

To begin we need a low bass sound such as a drum or our hands clapping to break through the denser vibrations. Think of how you feel when you hear a deep bass beat, perhaps from a passing car with the stereo on too loud or at a nightclub. We can feel this deep bass vibrate through our physical body, shaking up the stagnation within us. It is the same experience for the fabric of our home. The drumming or clapping literally breaks up the old memory vibrations absorbed by the bricks and mortar of your space.

Then the different bells and chimes begin to attune the space to a higher, more refined vibration. Think of church bells calling people to service on a Sunday. We can hear how the purity of a bell tone or a chime clarifies a space.

Finally, white sage and Nitraj incense are sacred herbs that have been recognized as having healing properties and are excellent at expelling negative environmental energies. The herb smoke penetrates places where the other sounds cannot go and the smoke is a natural connection to spirit as it mingles with the air. The sacred smoke is a refinement and can be omitted if you wish.

Now you understand the principles of the process, if you cannot locate any item, improvise. The technique outlined here is a ritualistic and powerful ceremonial way to deeply clear your home, but it's by no means the only way. For example, you could open all the doors and windows and play loud rock music for five minutes to blast out the stagnant energies, followed by closing the windows and playing some choir music or other suitably refined classical music to raise the vibration of the space.

1. Before you begin, write a list of your intentions for the space. Make them positive, state them as if you already have them and be specific; for example, 'Thank you for the restorative, healing sleep and the clearly remembered dreams when I wake.' There is no limit to the number of intentions you can have.

2. Do space clearing when you feel physically, emotionally and mentally fit. Avoid it if you are pregnant, ill, menstruating or have an open wound, as your personal energy will be depleted at these times. It will be focused on healing your body or nourishing the foetus and we need to be physically strong when space clearing.

3. Choose a day for the ceremony. New moons are excellent for bringing in new opportunities and full moons are better for letting go of what is no longer working in your life. (*See Resources for an excellent moon calendar you can download.*)

4. For maximum benefit, clear clutter first, physically clean your home, vacuum and empty all rubbish bins.

5. Put fresh flowers around your home, honour your space and make it beautiful. Remember this is ultimately about honouring *you*!

6. Clear away food and drink from exposed surfaces or put them in sealed containers.

7. Remove all jewellery, as metal can absorb environmental energies.

8. Cleanse yourself before you begin. Preferably take a bath or shower. At the very minimum, wash your face and hands.

9. Work alone and in silence. (Babies and small children should definitely not be present, as they can be over-sensitive to clearing toxins.)

10. Open a door or window.

11. Gather everything you need (candle, drum, incense or smudge stick, bells or chimes, sea salt) and create a specific place to work from. Effectively, you are creating a mini-altar in whichever way feels appropriate to you.

12. Light a candle and spend some time meditating on what you want from your space and your *intentions* for clearing it. Spend a few minutes grounding your energy and doing some deep breathing techniques. Reaffirm your intention, call it out loud into the space.

13. Put a line of salt across the entrance of each door to the outside world, for example the front and back door and any patio doors. Leave it in place for 24 hours before vacuuming. (This soaks up the negative energy.)

14. Walk round your home clapping or drumming (if you have a drum), loudly as you go.

15. Do another circuit ringing a bell or Tibetan chimes. These vibrate on a higher frequency and are useful for fine-tuning the vibrations. (This can be replaced with choral or classical music if you don't have a bell.)

16. Walk round your home once more, burning a white sage smudge stick or a Nitraj incense stick. Waft the smoke around the inner circumference of your home, making sure to pay particular attention to any dark corners. (You light the sage or incense stick, then blow out the flame

to create the smoke.) Take a dish with you to collect any falling ash.

17. Wash your hands to clear any negative energies from them and close the windows.

18. Stand at your front door looking in and imagine a white bubble of light completely encircling your home. Your home is now clear and protected.

19. Walk round one last time, calling out your list of goals and any other feel-good emotions you'd like to fill your home with, for example laughter, joy or love.

20. Safely burn your list of goals (a saucepan is good for this). Collect the ash and put it in the soil of a houseplant or in your garden. Water it well and watch your dreams grow into reality.

21. Expect miracles!

You may like to play your favourite music once a space clearing has been completed to enhance the positive vibrations felt in your space. Drink plenty of water (at least two litres) on the day of space clearing and finish with a sea salt or Epsom salt bath.

The physical results of detoxing our homes are similar to those experienced from a detox diet, i.e. headache, feeling drained and tired and irritable. This will only last a short while (48 hours maximum) before the new revitalized energy kicks in.

If you've taken some action on this chapter, however small, you'll already have noticed how your dreams have increased, either in number or intensity, and/or your ability to recall them has improved. That's how responsive dreams are. They want our attention – they thrive on it!

Now you have some good dream material and going to bed is pleasurable, let's get on with the exciting task of working those dreams!

CHAPTER THREE

The Dream Gym

Improving our Dream Muscles

'Do not go where the path may lead. Go instead where there is no path and leave a trail.'
Ralph Emerson

OK, it's time to get to work. I can guide you, encourage you, inspire you, even improve your technique, but I can't dream for you. If you want access to that extraordinary genius inside, then you'll need to get in the dream gym and work out. It's the only way – there are no short cuts. Still, at least this is a gym where the most strenuous activity required is lying in bed, picking up a pen and paper and writing down your dreams.

Our dreaming mind is a muscle that we need to build up in order to get optimum results. When we embark on a physical fitness programme we don't immediately get fit, it takes time. It is the application of regular practice that eventually makes the difference, turning our flab into sleek, toned muscle. The same is true of our dreams.

With dreams, though, it's a cinch – there are no sweaty bodies or muscle-bound egos to encounter (unless, of course, they're in our dreams!). We can build our dreaming potential in the privacy of our own minds; it's exciting, always different, potentially life-changing, mostly fun, and we can practise every night for free. What could be better than that?

Dreams are nebulous, fluid and flowing. Their meaning isn't always immediately apparent, so we need to build trust in them. Practising the exercises in this book will collect the evidence you need to prove to yourself that there is phenomenal intelligence in the dreaming mind. Until we begin to record our dreams, though, this intelligence doesn't become fully apparent. A one-off dream is great and useful in its own right, but with a series of dreams the true power of self-knowledge emerges.

Dream Assessment

If you join a gym, you'll be given a fitness assessment to help you work out where you're at and how to train to get the results you want. This next exercise helps us assess where our current dreaming attention is likely to be focused and will help us recognize what our dreams are trying to tell us.

THE DREAM OF LIFE WHEEL

On a scale of 1–10 , where 1 is bad and 10 great, please write in the appropriate circle below how this area of your life is now. Work intuitively, going with the first number that comes into your head.

9. STATUS; PLACEMENT IN SOCIAL HIERARCHY; RELATIONSHIP TO PEERS. Do you feel your worth is recognized in the world? Are you valued and well paid for what you do?

2. RELATIONSHIPS WITH YOUR SPOUSE, PARTNER, BUSINESS PARTNER; BOSS, ETC. Do you argue constantly or consider yourself part of a well-functioning team? Are you single and happy with that or are you looking for love? Are you happily married?

4. WEALTH; LUCK; FORTUNATE BLESSINGS. Do you consider yourself a lucky person or do you feel everyone has more luck than you?

3. RELATIONSHIPS WITH FAMILY MEMBERS, PARENTS, GRANDPARENTS, SIBLINGS, TEACHERS, MENTORS. Do you get on well with your family? Did you hate school ? Do you speak to your parents?

8. PERSONAL DEVELOPMENT; MEDITATION; SPIRITUAL DEVELOPMENT. Do you know what makes you tick? Do you spend quality time with yourself?

1. CAREER PROGRESSION; JOURNEY IN LIFE. Do you love what you do? Are you stuck in a rut?

6. HELPFUL FRIENDS AND NEIGHBOURS; CHARITY; COMMUNITY SERVICE. Are you willing to lend a hand when needed? Are there always friends on tap when you need them?

7. CREATIVITY; CHILDREN; IDEAS; PROJECTS. Are you fully expressing yourself? Do you love your children? Are you experiencing difficulties conceiving?

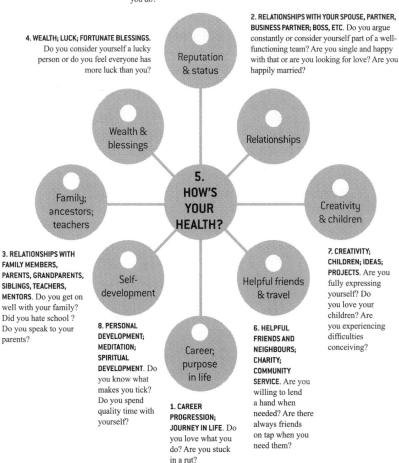

Reputation & status

Wealth & blessings

Relationships

Family; ancestors; teachers

5. HOW'S YOUR HEALTH?

Creativity & children

Self-development

Helpful friends & travel

Career; purpose in life

Now take your three lowest scores and notice which areas of your life they fall in. Measure these life areas against the themes of any dreams that are already showing up for you. If you're new to dreams, keep these scores to refer back to once you start to accumulate dream material.

One of the roles of the dreaming mind is to correct our emotional imbalances. So you may already see a correlation between the areas that are not working in your life and the dreams you are having. What are your dreams telling you to do about this situation? What are the negative emotions present in your dreams that need resolving? We'll work on how you can easily resolve these issues later. For now, just observe any patterns you can see beginning to emerge.

Everything in the universe has an equal and opposite energy. Our job is keeping in balance. To do this, large pendulum swings either way won't help. It is the tiny incremental shifts between any two opposing forces that lead to the illusion of perfect balance – illusion, because in truth balance is only possible through perpetual motion, constant correcting and counter-correcting, our dreams balancing our daytime world and our daytime balancing our dreams.

This dream of life wheel can be seen to have a similar energy. If we are on purpose in life (career/purpose in life), then we will naturally achieve the remuneration and recognition we deserve (reputation and status). If we have a good relationship with our family, we tend to pass on that experience in good parenting to our own offspring (creativity and children). If we have good teachers and foundations, we go on to realize our own creative genius. If we're independent and emotionally intelligent within our self (self-development), then we're likely to attract healthy relationships with others. If we have helpful friends, we're likely to be able to gain more wealth and feel generally more blessed in life. Health lies on its own in the centre. It's the emptiness in the middle of the wheel that makes it work. Without good health and vitality it's impossible to achieve success and balance in the other areas.

Now look at the exact opposite energy of the three lowest scores you picked. How is that area faring in relation to your current struggles? Are you overcompensating in one area at the expense of another? What changes do you need to make to correct this imbalance?

Intention

The results we get in life are not just about the actions we take but also about the intent behind those actions. If we don't pay heed to our intentions, we tend to experience haphazard results. So start with intending to remember your dreams clearly and the results will follow. And as you begin to pay more attention to the dreams you do remember, you will remember more.

We can actually reduce the need for action to a minimum by allowing ourselves to focus on what we desire until we feel the positive energy begin to move within us. This process of intent is applicable to all areas of our life, not just our dreams. When we focus our intent on what we want rather than what we don't want, that's where our energy flows and the universe conspires to support our intent, and right action becomes effortless. Of course, this intent has to be pure desire, not energy based on fear, anxiety or need. Luckily, by the time you get to the end of this book you'll have the tools to clear out those nasties because if they're present you can guarantee they'll be turning up in your dreams!

Dare to Dream

Daring to dream and daring to believe in our dreams 100 per cent are the key to intent.

I am reminded of a client of mine who was desperate to have a baby and needed IVF treatment. She was telling me she felt positive but obviously didn't want to get her hopes up in case she was disappointed. I stopped her at this point. This process was going to take months and she was never going to give herself that 100 per cent chance to go for what she truly wanted. Despite there being apparently low statistics in terms of the likelihood of success (I think it was 14 per cent), the bottom line was she would either be pregnant after the treatment or she wouldn't. So she had a 50 per cent chance of it working or not working. But she was already suffering with the possibility of loss by not allowing herself to believe fully in the possibility of success.

This is an extreme example, but we're all doing it to a greater or lesser extent, constantly projecting ourselves into the past or the future and finding it impossible to stay centred in the present. How often do we repress our feelings and experiences in an effort to avoid the pain of disappointment or loss?

As we know, energy flows where our attention goes. So it is far better to focus our energy on increasing the statistical probability of a positive outcome. If it doesn't work, we can deal with that outcome when it arrives, but at least we'll know we gave ourselves the best possible chance of success.

We do not reach wholeness by sitting and waiting for healing to come to us. There is always the element of the hero's quest, the journey, the pilgrimage, the search for answers – even if it's just ringing a therapist or looking up a number for help. In engaging with your Dream Whisperer, you inspire yourself, you dare to dream, you give yourself permission to travel through the gateway of the unknown. Through that portal of the mind that can unfold the great mystery and teach you all you need to know.

Dreams whisper to us constantly. Capture those whispers when you can. Even vivid dreams can be reduced to mist within minutes. They cling tantalizingly to the outskirts of our mind but we can't grasp them, pull them back. Then occasionally a moment in the day will trigger total or partial recall and the dream breaks through to our conscious awareness with surprising clarity. Seize those moments and record them. The more dreams you have to play with, the more fun and useful the whole process becomes. Soon you'll be wondering why you didn't pay attention to your dreams before, they are so rich in personal anecdote and reasoning.

So, dare to dream. Set your intention to engage with your dreams. Embark on the quest for healing.

And now we're clear on where we're headed, let's warm up those dormant dream muscles.

The Warm-Up – Dreams Respond to Attention

Warming up our dreaming attention is predominantly about becoming more aware of our dreams – engaging with them, consciously recognizing that they are a vital necessity in our lives, as important as eating, breathing and exercising. You'll discover that your dream life responds quickly to any level of attention and will, with minimal effort, soon be providing you with gratifyingly rich material to work with. Just reading this book will lead to more dreams, as it filters your interest in the subject to your extremely receptive unconscious mind!

In fact, when we pay attention to anything in life, it starts to show up. There is a straightforward neurological reason for this phenomenon: the reticular activating system of the brain, or RAS. We've all had an experience of this. Perhaps the easiest way to illustrate is when you are considering purchasing a new car or have just brought a new model. Before you decided on which car to buy you hadn't even been aware of this type of car, but now you see it everywhere, even in your chosen colour. Your brain now recognizes the colour and model and has created a search mechanism to locate that aspect in the world.

RAS ACTIVATION EXERCISE

To illustrate this mechanism further, play this game with a partner or friend. Ask them to look around the room you're sitting in and memorize the number of *green* items that they can see. Let them spend a couple of minutes doing this, really focusing on remembering all the *green* items.

Then ask them to close their eyes and tell you how many *brown* items they recall from the same room. They'll find this hard if not impossible to do, yet if you both now check back in the room, there are probably many brown items.

The reason they have not been able to 'see' the brown items is because their attention has been focused on the green items.

This is how we create our individual reality. We will quite literally only see the things we spend time focusing on. This idea obviously has a myriad of implications in our life and it is also how the dreaming mind operates. When we start to pay attention to our dreams, they turn up. They've always been there, it's just that we didn't notice them before and now we do.

We can increase our dreaming attention further by reading articles on dreams, searching for dream topics on the internet, discussing our dreams with friends and family, engaging in the daydreaming techniques we'll discuss later and, most important of all, *writing our dreams down*. We'll come back to this in a minute, as it is the most fundamental factor in building our dream muscles. It's the cardio part of class – we may not like doing it, as it seems like hard work, but we know it's essential for our fitness so we get on and push through. All these simple techniques will keep your unconscious mind tuned in. It's like a radio antenna tuned into the dream frequency, allowing you to pick up the dream channel.

It does take effort to acquire our own dream appreciation knowledge. Nevertheless, I believe the rewards far outweigh the input required. All the techniques given here are designed to build our deep dream appreciation fast. Still, this isn't about engaging with every dream, unless of course you want to. Dreams will do their own thing anyway in that they will continue to occur, file memories, process emotions and teach us things whether we pay conscious attention to them or not.

There are lots of dream processes and exercises throughout the book that can be done over a short period whilst you're on holiday or over a long weekend, for example. You can organize your own dream retreat specifically geared to receiving a particularly useful answer or insight into some problem. Or you can work with those dreams that absolutely startle you awake and stay with you for days, or the ones that keep recurring, and of course any nightmares. Our dreams will always be there, waiting for us to choose to engage. We can become dreaming triathletes or just lose a bit of emotional flab and tone up our creative genius. It's entirely up to us how far or deep we go in exploring our dreaming attention.

Some people may consider engaging with our dreams is whimsical or indulgent. I believe it is an act of self-love and not to appreciate them is tantamount to self-neglect. In my study with the Quechua shamans of Peru I was taught a valuable lesson in this respect: 'You cannot serve another until you serve yourself.' As beings of modern cultures we tend to struggle with this idea. We're taught it is selfish to put ourselves first. Far from it – we are selfish not to, as only by serving ourselves do we have the energy, time and compassion required to help another.

Good Gym Techniques Improve Dream Recall

Some people say they never dream; others say that they can't remember their dreams. But we all definitely dream. Sleep research has proven that – well, as far as it can, bearing in mind that the only way to investigate whether someone is dreaming or not is to wake them up and ask them!

Even those of us who think we don't really dream or rarely remember our dreams will still have a handful of them where the experience was so emotionally powerful and vivid it really shouted at us from the unconscious, and that shout will stay with us forever. I had a recurring dream as a child about visiting my grandparents' house and finding three half-barrels sitting outside. Under the third barrel was a huge hairy rat that leaped out and tore the throat out of my stepfather in a gruesome close-up image. I can still remember the intensity of image and feeling of that dream as though it happened last night, though it took place over 30 years ago. Yet I'd be hard pushed to remember a 'real' event that could induce such intensity in me.

Often we don't remember dreams because we don't give ourselves those precious few moments in the morning to absorb them. That's when they are whispering to us, tugging at the corners of our mind, making themselves subtly felt. The quickest way to better dream recall is to lie still upon waking and stay inside, eyes closed, reflecting on how you're feeling, what you're thinking about. Those of you who currently think you can't remember your dreams will be stunned by how much information is actually available if you lie still and listen to the whispers of the night.

A simple adjustment of your sleep habits can often provoke dreams – or rather, their recall. Remember you will only remember your dreams if woken during the REM cycle. Dreams in other sleep stages are rare and generally less creative or meaningful in content.

Here are the best techniques for consciously remembering more dreams:

1. Take a glass of water to bed. Drink half of it before retiring, saying, 'I will remember my dreams.' When you wake up, drink the rest of it, saying, 'Now I remember my

dreams.' It works because water holds memory, and we are in large part water, therefore the water will trigger the memory of the dream, either in the moment or later in the day.

2. We already know intention is key. Set the intention as you drift off to sleep: 'I will clearly remember my dreams.'

3. Lie still on waking with your eyes closed. Tune into yourself. Ask, 'What am I feeling?' 'Where was I just now?' What was I thinking?' Generally this is enough to at least start to bring snippets of the dream back, even if it is nothing more than a feeling right now or a fleeting image. With practice, this quickly builds to full dream recall.

4. Write your dreams down! More on how to do that below.

This is generally enough to get the recall muscle activated in most of us. Maybe we won't be recalling dreams every night – that takes time and practice to build up – but certainly one or two full dreams and other fragments per week.

You can also try the Limelight Essence called 'Dream Fairies'. It was developed specifically to improve dream recall and I always get excellent dreams on the nights I remember to take it (*see Resources for stockists*).

Those of you who are still dreamless after a couple of weeks might like to try some of these more extreme techniques, which are all about catching that elusive REM dream wave:

1. Snooze buttons are marvellous dreaming aides. Set the alarm for an hour earlier, then just keep pressing 'snooze'.

2. Set your alarm for two hours earlier than you want to get up and then reset it for half-hourly intervals.

3. You could try randomly setting two to three alarms to go off at spaced intervals throughout the night.

4. If all else fails, drink at least a litre of water just before bed. (I did say these were extreme measures.)

5. If you have night-owl friends, get them to call you one and a half hours after you go to sleep.

Write It Down — Make It Happen!

The simple act of recording our dreams allows us to be influenced by them instinctively, even if we do nothing with them. There's huge power in making something as nebulous as our dreams conscious through the act of writing them down. By doing this we have engaged our dreaming attention. We have initiated a relationship between our conscious and our unconscious minds, even if we don't yet fully understand it.

Developing the discipline to record our dreams is the best gift we can give ourselves. If you do nothing else, please train yourself into the habit of writing dreams down. A well-used dream journal will be the biggest gift to yourself you've ever invested in. This one essential key unlocks all the dreaming doors to truly knowing ourselves. This is the basic muscle we need to tone to release the genius within.

Many books have been written about the magic of writing things down, and the basic idea is equally applicable to dreams. Taking something from the world of our mind and giving it a physical reality in terms of words on paper carries an energy of manifestation. Things will start to happen, seemingly of their own accord. Yet if we do periodically review our dreams, we'll see that all the clues were there.

How to Record your Dreams

There are a number of different ways to record your dreams. Some methods suit some people better than others and it is for each of us to decide which works for us. Whatever method you use, it needs to be easily accessible at the moment that you wake. If you jump out of bed, go to the loo, get a cup of tea or start running over the day ahead in your mind, you will lose valuable dream detail, if not the whole dream.

The simplest and probably the easiest method of recording your dreams is a dream journal by the side of the bed. With it should be a pen and preferably a night light. Often really significant dreams turn up when we wake in the middle of the night and it's best not to disturb our partners too often if we value marital harmony! Therefore some kind of small reading light will allow you to record the dream with minimal disturbance to anyone else.

With nocturnal dreams, I tend to sneak off to the loo and scribble them down. As it's the middle of the night and I'm still half dreaming, it works fine. If you wait until morning, despite how vivid and real the dream feels at 3 a.m., you will inevitably forget it. There are endless examples of people losing valuable information by doing that, myself included. I once awoke from a vivid dream about winning a very large amount on the lottery. I had clearly seen the six winning numbers. However, not being disciplined in recording dreams at the time, I lost the numbers in the short time it took me to get up and find pen and paper. Who's to say whether those numbers would have won? Often such a dream is pure wish-fulfilment, but I'd like to have given myself the chance to find out!

As an alternative to pen and paper you can use a digital voice recorder. This is quick and easy and for complex dreams can be a real bonus. The disadvantage is that you need to get the files transcribed for it to be useful and that can take time. My ultimate in dream luxury would be to record my dreams for speed and convenience and then have them transcribed for me.

You could even type your dreams straight onto the computer, although you're in danger of losing dream details by doing this. The advantage of our technological age, though, is that the computer is a fabulous tool for being able to search and cross-reference your dream signs and symbols, which is an essential process in creating our own dream dictionaries. It also enables you to easily find a dream if you can remember a key word or phrase or the title.

There is something special inherent in the act of writing and on balance it is my preferred method, but it does take discipline to do, at least until it has become embedded as a new habit. It is well documented that it takes 28 days to change a habit (which interestingly is the length of one moon cycle). Consequently, set the intention that you will keep an initial dream journal for 28 days, as this will install the new habit in you. By the time you get to review this 28-day dream series you'll be so blown away by what you've discovered, I can guarantee you'll want to continue.

You don't have to remember your dreams every night for it to work; it's about practice. Whatever you get, write it down – a fragment, an emotion, a feeling, a word, even sometimes 'I know I've been dreaming but I can't remember any of it.' This isn't about perfection, it truly is about practice. There's no perfect way of doing this and there's no destination. They're your dreams, this is your journey – your own unique and magical unfolding.

This is how I trained myself. In childhood I was full of dreams, mostly nightmares from which I'd wake shaking and terrified. As a young adult I was not a naturally prolific dreamer. Left to its own devices my dreaming mind didn't often wake me up with a dream I could remember. I learned to recall my dreams when I started asking for dreams in relation to houses I was working on as a *feng shui* consultant. Since my more formal investigation into the nature of dreams in latter years, my dreaming ability has increased exponentially. I dream regularly now and can easily program my mind to receive a dream when I need one. So, if I can go from being one of those people who said 'Oh, I never remember my dreams' to dreaming nightly, so can you.

What to Capture in your Journal

It's not essential to remember a whole dream for it to be useful – even fragments can be helpful. Dreams whisper to us in snatches. They may involve a joke, a pun, a play on words, perhaps a certain number or particular timing. They provoke our sexual awareness; they challenge our beliefs about what's possible. They are moments of truth. They are also illusory and fantastical.

I prefer to use a plain-paged journal rather than lined. As I tend to write many dreams in semi-darkness, it helps if I don't need to write between the lines! If I don't have time to write down all the connecting elements of a dream and I want to capture the details I will mind map the dream, putting the title I give it in the centre and letting the scenes branch off from there. I will also draw out any symbols or shapes of other odd things I see in my dreams.

Here's a checklist to help you:

Key Dream Journal Elements

* Date the page. Be consistent in the date you use, as we generally go to sleep on one day and awake on another. I use the date of the day I'm going to sleep in. This works for me as I usually write my dreaming intention down in my journal before sleeping.

* Give your dream a name, a title, something that captures its essence. Make it memorable and relevant. Think movie titles and tabloid headlines. Sometimes simply naming the dream can trigger its meaning. It also helps you remember and find the dream in a handwritten journal.

* After the title, jot any key words or phrases that jumped out of the dream at you. We tend to forget dreaming language fast, so capture this first.

* On the right-hand page only, write your dream in the present tense, as though you were re-experiencing it. Even if it's just a fragment, write it down. Include as much detail as possible. What senses were present – taste, colour, smell, feel, sound? What were the emotions you experienced in this dream? How did you feel when you

Terror Attack Dream

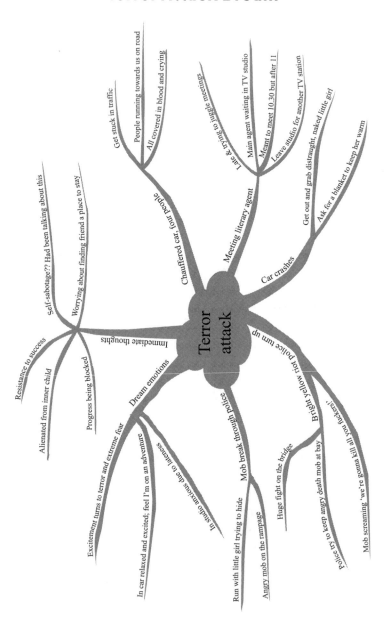

woke up from it? Use drawings or mind maps if it helps. Go through the dream and underline (in a different-coloured pen for easier searching) any symbols that stand out or seem significant in some way, including their adjectives, for example 'old house', 'large oak tree', 'sick man', 'blue aeroplane', 'right leg', 'scary monster'. On the left-hand side jot down any immediate associations that spring to mind as you underline the symbols. We'll come back to these symbols later.

✳ Use the left-hand page to document briefly your current reality, for example, 'Having a hard time with my husband. We're both working too hard. Got home early from work and watched *The Lion King* with the kids.' Sometimes it's good to write this first part in your journal the night before. It helps attune your dreaming attention to the issues at hand. Now jot down any immediate insights or connections with your current life you can see in relation to the dream. Leave space for other insights that may come to you throughout the day.

Trust

The gateway to our dreams is to trust, to surrender to the unknown. Each night when we fall asleep, we do this. We're completely vulnerable, forced to surrender to our dreaming minds, our bodies paralysed, chemicals switched on and off – nothing is under our control. It's extraordinary that we allow ourselves to go there, that the mechanism is created in such a way that it makes us feel safe to go to sleep, to enter into the dream state.

But we need to trust not only in allowing ourselves to dream but also in what our dreams are saying to us. Here's a simple three-step process for building trust in your dreaming mind:

BUILDING TRUST

* Set your intention. As you fall asleep, simply enquire of your dreaming mind: 'What do I most need to know right now?'

* Give yourself permission to journey into the unknown. Allow yourself to go there. Trust, surrender to yourself. Trust that you will receive whatever information you most need.

* Write down everything that happens!

Trust in the process – it will not fail you. The Dream Whisperer will happily oblige you with the perfect answer whilst you slumber. I use this process a lot to keep my life on track and in flow. We'll get on to unlocking the magic of *what* you capture in Chapters Five and Six, but for now gather the dream evidence.

Optimizing Performance

A Time and a Place

Remembering dreams and working with them constructively needs to fit in with where we're at in life. For example, those of you with small children or newborn babies will obviously be losing out, not only on sleep but dreams too, as you're woken by the little ones demanding attention and the whispers of the night-time are lost. Enjoy your sleep when you can get it and accept that this isn't going to be a period when you're going to remember and record lots of dreams. Your dreaming mind will catch up when it needs to.

The same goes for anyone else currently experiencing a lifestyle that radically interferes with the ability to enjoy dream appreciation. You can always employ the daydream techniques found throughout this book, though (*see pages 76 and 236*), and new parents can benefit greatly from power naps (*see page 232*).

The Dream Diet

There are many myths relating to certain substances increasing our dream recall. Late-night cheese eating, alcohol, cigarettes, chocolate and caffeine have all variously been reported as causing more dreams and in particular nightmares. There is nothing intrinsic in any of these substances that will lead to increased dreaming. In fact, alcohol abuse, along with cannabis, is a well-documented dream depressant. However, substances that are stimulants or hard for the body to digest late at night, like cheese, do disturb our sleep patterns, meaning we'll have a higher likelihood of waking during one of those all-important REM phases and hence we appear to dream more after consuming them.

To improve the quality of your sleep and dreams, it is best to avoid such substances for at least two to three hours before retiring. Drink camomile tea and avoid late-night snacks of any sort, with the exception of bananas. These contain a substance that helps promote a good night's sleep.

We'll know our time in the dream gym has been successful because positive changes will start to occur – in our behaviour, in our life, in our interaction with others and in how we develop. They will become obvious to us, and the more we practise in the dream gym, the easier and more obvious they will become, and soon we'll find ourselves thoroughly enjoying the game and wondering how we managed to live a life without considering our dreams!

Now we know how to dream and how to remember dreams and record them, it's time to get better acquainted with our dreaming mind.

CHAPTER FOUR

Mind the Gap

Getting your Minds Talking to Each Other

'That's what learning is, understanding something we've always understood – but in a new way.'
Doris Lessing

To enable our dream work to become easy and effortless we need a model of the mind to hang our dreaming hat on. The one I'm choosing is from the Peruvian cosmological vision of the world, as I've studied it in depth. However, as you will see, it has many correspondences with more modern interpretations of the mind.

A Model of the Mind

In Peruvian cosmology there are three worlds: the lower world, the middle world and the upper world. This trio, amongst other associations, corresponds to the unconscious mind, the conscious mind and the Higher Self respectively.

We can see this idea of the trinity replicated everywhere, from the populist idea of mind, body, spirit to Christianity's Father, Son and Holy Ghost, Freud's idea of the id, ego and superego, and Jung's unconscious, conscious and superconscious minds.

Here we're talking about functions of the mind and the structure of our mental landscape, not physical parts of the brain. There is also no inferred hierarchy within these levels of the mind. They're all equally required for optimum well-being.

In order to know ourselves and access our true inspiration, we need to be able to communicate with the Higher Self, and we can only do this via the unconscious mind, the home of our dreams. So we need to build good rapport between our conscious and unconscious minds, and that is what we'll be focusing on in this chapter.

When the relationship between the conscious and unconscious minds is working well, the Dream Whisperer can usher in the inspirations of the Higher Self and we get to consult our own internal oracle – an oracle that has the power to solve any problem, overcome any obstacle and achieve any goal we can set for ourselves. To unlock this power we need to understand the relationship between these minds and their roles and functions.

The Higher Self

The Higher Self just is. It could be viewed as the aspect of us that is the mind of God experiencing itself. It has no judgement and thinks we're totally perfect, as, at the highest level, we are.

This mind can give us exactly what we want, *but* it has to be asked. This is essential to understand. The dreaming mind is one route in, one of the golden keys that allows the inspiration of the Higher Self to be channelled through to our waking reality, to our conscious self. The lesson of life is to raise the physical to the spiritual. The lesson of mastery is to bring the spiritual down into the physical, and this we can do through our dreams.

The Higher Self takes care of itself. Its guidance is available to us 24/7 if we know how to translate the messages. So we need to focus our attention on the other two minds. It is in this relationship that the power of our dreams lies.

The Conscious Mind

The conscious mind is that part of us that actively has thoughts we know and understand. It is the mind we use to speak and communicate with, the mind where we actively engage in the processes of analysis and logical, rational thought. It is also where the ego resides.

Our conscious mind has free will. One of its jobs is to teach the unconscious mind what to focus on – that is, to contemplate and focus on what we want, for example better health, better relationships and more money.

Of course, at one level, knowing ourselves consciously is simply identifying with some ideas rather than others. We each have our own unique filter system from which we consciously take data in from the universe and decide what it means to us. This enables us to make conscious sense of our reality and from it we create our beliefs. These beliefs create our experience. Everything has to go through our filters. However, therein lies an inherent problem. What if our filters are faulty? Our perception of events incorrect? This is where our dreams come in. Dreams alert us to our faulty perceptions or erroneous emotional responses, or simply tell us where we're going wrong and how to put it right.

The Unconscious Mind

Our unconscious meanwhile takes in everything else that we consciously miss or filter out in order to function in everyday reality. It would be too much for us to know everything at once. We'd be like rabbits caught in the headlights, stupefied by all those trillions of microscopic electrochemical interactions that cause us to fizz and pop in and out of existence every moment of every day.

This power behind the throne, the unconscious mind, is where our route to wholeness lies. Antony Robbins dubbed it 'the giant within'. It is constantly absorbing and processing data with an overall intention, a reasoning behind the mayhem: to bring us into balance, to return us to a homoeostatic state. Everything in our biological, chemical, energetic make-up works that way. So why would our dreams be any different? They are mechanisms by which we continually reorganize our psyche and bring it back into balance.

The unconscious mind wants to please your conscious mind; it wants to please you. It takes everything you say and think as a suggestion upon which it acts. It doesn't have independent will or creativity; it follows the rules of the conscious mind. So it needs to be consistently told what to do in a clear, unambiguous way.

Communicating with the unconscious mind and the world of our dreams enables us to have more control and certainty about who we are and what we're doing here. The unconscious mind controls so much of our external behaviour that being able to understand and relate to it in a meaningful way is profound and potentially life-changing. It shifts our perspective and allows us to glimpse between the worlds, to see what we already know deep within our hearts: the essence of our immortal nature. To paraphrase the psychologist and master dream interpreter Carl Jung, 'Until we make the unconscious conscious it will control our lives and we will call it fate.'

Teamwork

We can better understand the relationship between our unconscious and conscious minds by thinking of a large global corporation, Me, Inc. The boss of the company represents our conscious mind. They're the driving vision of the company. They don't deal with details or the 'hows and whys', they focus on the 'whats and wheres'. They decide on where the company needs to go, what profits it needs to make. They're in command of the big picture, the overview. They can't possibly know or retain all the smaller day-to-day activities that allow the company to function and grow. That's the job of the unconscious mind, or the workforce.

When the boss decides on a goal for the company, they pass their instruction to the workforce to implement the strategy. If they have communicated their vision well, in alignment with their and the company's values and resources, then the company goal will be fulfilled. If the workforce is unable to comply, they will report to the boss, telling them why. Perhaps there's not enough workforce or there are faults in the system or further investment is required or the goal is against the ethos of the company. The workforce will also offer various suggestions on how to solve these issues.

Our minds work in the same way. It is the role of the conscious mind to set the goal. It is the role of the unconscious mind to work out how to get the goal. If the unconscious mind can't achieve the goal or solve the problem, then it will let the conscious mind know through the feedback mechanism of our dreams.

Unfortunately our conscious mind can't hold all its beliefs in mind at once and we get what we believe in life, not the goals we set. Our dreams are excellent indicators of what those underlying beliefs are. One of the most beneficial roles they play is in illustrating what we're choosing to ignore whilst awake. If we're not living in harmony with ourselves and our values, our dreams soon let us know in displays of fear, anxiety or otherwise negatively orientated emotions.

Fear and anxiety are warnings from our unconscious mind that we're not focusing on what we want. Anxiety is always about something that hasn't happened yet, some future event that hasn't occurred.

Dreams let us know when we're on the right path, too, as this one from the author and journalist Anna Pasternak illustrates:

I was in the car with a male friend. He was driving me to see a large new house. This house wasn't in an area I would have chosen and it was over £1 million and in the dream it seemed a lot of money but I could afford it and he said I could save £500,000 VAT, so it seemed a bargain! Then suddenly he leaned across and took my fingers in his hand and squeezed them. It was such an electric, erotic and meaningful gesture that in the dream I was mid-sentence and my heart was beating so fast that I couldn't finish it. I squeezed his hand back and there was so much unspoken feeling in the gesture. There was so much promise as we toyed with each other's fingers.

Anna was contemplating a move to New York, perhaps not somewhere she would have previously considered or 'chosen', but it seemed a bargain and taking action was full of 'promise'. The underlying sexual tension in this dream is indicative of our primal animal nature, the desire that motivates us into action. Anna's unconscious seemed to support her conscious decision in this instance.

The Rules We Make Up

Our experience of the world is determined by our ideas about it. So if we want to change things in our life we need to change our beliefs or assumptions. Often our beliefs are unconscious. This next exercise allows you to test those unconscious beliefs against your conscious desires and to calibrate them for congruency. You can use this exercise to test where you're at and also, if used regularly, it will clear out any negative beliefs that are preventing you from manifesting your dreams.

DREAM TESTER

* Think of a dream you would like to manifest. For this exercise we are going to use happiness as an example.

* Close your eyes, take some long, slow, quiet breaths and relax. (*If you need help with relaxing, use the exercise on page 37.*)

* Imagine an entirely clear landscape before you. This landscape reflects how much happiness and satisfaction you can have in your life.

* Let that happiness be represented by a clear blue sky. Anything less than perfect happiness is represented by dust, smog and clouds.

* Add a dial at the side to measure the sky. What percentage of blue sky is it registering?

* Now concentrate and determine to increase the amount of blue sky. Watch the dial increase and notice how you feel in your body. You're watching for small subtle changes in the physical self, for example tightness in the stomach or chest area, a change in temperature or pain anywhere. Be with these sensations and send loving kindness to them with your mind. Imagine smiling into the discomfort, accepting it fully in order to give it the chance to change.

* Now let the sky and the dial return to the starting percentage and feel your body relax back to normal.

Open your eyes, stretch and come back to normal awareness.

You can repeat this exercise with any area of your life you'd like to check. Do it daily, gradually increasing the percentage on the dial in line with the comfort of your body until you can feel perfectly at ease with the dial at 100 per cent.

Taking Responsibility

Dreams give us guidance, not definitive answers. Our conscious mind is the one that has the choice as to whether to act on the information of the dream. But we need to allow ourselves to accept the reality of the unconscious as a valid partner in our lives, to understand that working together our two minds create a powerful partnership and dreams are the language of that partnership.

To know our true selves we need to be able to translate this dream language. Just because we don't understand Chinese we don't assume that what is spoken in Chinese is rubbish, yet this tends to be how we respond to our dreams. At first glance, we have no idea what a dream means and therefore we dismiss it, whereas we can unlock the meaning simply by learning the language of our dreams, as we're doing now.

We live in a world of mirrors. We can know ourselves by interpreting the reality we inhabit. If someone's making us angry, where is that anger reflected inside ourselves? Remember we can't change another, but we can change ourselves. And the purpose of any relationship is to discover ourselves. It's not really anything to do with the other person. The same is true for dreams. By engaging with our dreams, we create a relationship not only between our conscious and unconscious minds but also with our Higher Self and our true power. Engaging with our dreams is an essential ingredient in being a well-balanced, healthy person.

In dreams, as with life, the responsibility for change always lies with the dreamer. It is not until we apply our knowledge that we gain understanding and wisdom. This is beautifully summed up by the following quote I read somewhere: 'Knowledge is knowing tomatoes are a fruit. Wisdom is knowing not to put them in a fruit salad.' The wisdom inside our dreams comes through a cooperative flow of energy and ideas crossing the bridge of dreaming between our conscious and unconscious minds. This is what leads to profound change.

For any process of change to work, a simple equation needs to exist: the problem plus resources equals a solution. In the context of dreams, our conscious mind has the problem, whilst our unconscious mind holds all the resources. Together they create the solution. The resulting dream is the source code for the solution. It is an active process of engaging our conscious mind with our dreaming mind in order to find that solution.

This relates to the old adage, 'If we keep doing what we've always done we'll keep getting what we've always got.' By connecting with the dreaming mind, we think new thoughts and allow our parameters of experience and the boundaries of our knowing to expand. This allows our conscious mind to have more awareness of our entire personality, our wholeness.

We're not actively engaging our dreams because we want control over our unconscious mind – we simply want to open the channels of communication between the minds.

Dancing with our Dreams

As with all evolving and learning, in making the journey from the present state to the desired state, we'll pass through a stage of confusion. Confusion is a good state – it means we're evolving and developing and it is always temporary. Where you're at right now probably doesn't make total sense, otherwise you wouldn't be reading this book about getting to know yourself through your dreams. For now, give yourself permission to be with confusion, knowing that eventually clarity will emerge.

One of the big issues with dream interpretation is that we don't always understand the differences between the conscious and unconscious minds. We get frustrated and confused by trying to apply logical analysis to what our dreaming mind has produced and it seems very meaningless. Dream analysis is very akin to the process of solving cryptic crossword clues. It's far easier, of course, because it's your own mind you're working with. You're not trying to second-guess the internal workings of the crossword compiler, because that compiler is you.

To extract meaningful information from our dreams we need to hear the whispers of meaning illustrated in the bizarre movies that play out in our mind. It is a far more fluid process than logical-thought processing allows for. We need to dance with our dreams, flirt with them. Then we will hear their sweet whisperings.

Our conscious mind tends to work in a linear fashion with information. It can apply reason and give contextual understanding to words and the accepted meaning associated with the usage of that word. For example, if we dream of a house, our conscious brain will take it quite literally as representing our house or some other house that we know. Yet our dreaming mind works symbolically, so in this instance a house can have a far broader context in relation to our life, i.e. it can represent a physical structure, foundations, including the physical body, the structure that houses our spirit, our psyche. Suddenly, a whole vista of new possibilities has opened up. That's why it's so important to go with your own interpretation of a symbol, but one that goes deeper than the literal meaning. We'll be learning how to do this in the next chapter.

Our daily perception of reality tends to be primarily based in the world of duality – a world where everything has an equal and opposite force. We understand and make sense of something in relation to its opposite. We know hot only in relation to cold, tall in relation to short, small in relation to large, the conscious mind in relation to the unconscious mind, and so on. But we miss out hugely on our potential in life if we're only willing to listen to the conscious rational part of ourselves without also investigating the creative intuitive side that lies buried in our unconscious minds. Dreams are the rulers of this realm. Certainly great artists, poets, scientists and philosophers throughout the ages have understood the power of dreams and harnessed that power to create masterpieces.

Hypnotic Dreaming

Most indigenous cultures have a different idea of dreams from us. They believe that everything's a dream. According to this view, we're living in a dream now. What we consider reality is but a consensual dream based on a fixed point of awareness, which gives us our homogenous view of the world. One of their key phrases is 'dreaming your dreams awake'. If we can understand the difference between what we perceive to be reality and what is a dream, then we can work with that to begin to create new dreams in our life. The vision quest of Native Americans and other native cultures is a way of accessing this hypnotic state of awareness where insight, visions and dreams can become manifest.

Hypnosis is another great way to build rapport between our conscious and unconscious minds, which leads fabulously into dreams, because the state between sleep and waking is itself hypnotic in nature.

The relationship between our two minds is closest and perhaps most easily understood during the two sleep phases we discussed in Chapter One, the hypnagogic and hypnopompic states. The prefix 'hypno' comes from the Greek word for sleep, *hypnos*. This is the basis of hypnosis, a state where our ego boundaries are loosened, we're more sensitive and can experience empathy with our environment. In that state, we're open to suggestibility, more creative in our processing and able to make lateral rather than linear associations. In other words, we're able to access that intuitive, creative side of ourselves that's brilliant at coming up with otherwise inaccessible solutions to our problems. This trance state allows us to both create and process dreams in a more productive way, and throughout this book we'll be using dream techniques that are designed to access this state.

Daydreaming Visions

Our real dreams can provide structures we're unable to create in waking reality, but our daydreams can access reasonable solutions that are still outside the realms of our conscious awareness. This is an area worth exploring to get quick easy access to creative solutions.

A daydreaming vision is an excellent process when contemplating a major change in lifestyle, perhaps getting married or changing career or deciding to have children or any other potentially huge decision we need to make. Generally when faced with such changes we talk to everyone – our families, friends, colleagues, advisors, etc. – seeking advice. Yet strangely, we rarely consult the one person who matters most: ourselves.

By taking ourselves out of our normal state of awareness and creating sensory deprivation in certain areas, we increase our sensory awareness in relation to our internal world. Without having to banish ourselves to splendid isolation for many days, we can replicate the creative magic of a vision quest in much less time. Of course, if you do have time, then a few days' retreat to a place of natural beauty will do wonders for your mind, body and soul!

DAYDREAMING QUEST

This quest reconnects you to your inner self, allowing you to seek advice from the one person that counts – you! It works best in an isolated place of nature but a local park or your back garden can work equally well, provided you will not be disturbed by people you know. I would suggest the absolute minimum time you set yourself for this is an hour, but longer periods are better. We carry a lot of tension, stress and baggage with us and it tends to take a while for us to relax enough to unload this before we can really get into what's underneath and what we're really feeling.

Good preparation will yield best results. Eat a light, healthy diet for a few days before your mini-retreat. At the very least, don't have any alcohol, caffeine, salt, dairy, processed foods or sugar. This helps clear your energy channels and allows your mind to be clearer to receive the insights you seek.

We already know *intent* is key. This is the first step. What is your intention? What do you most want guidance or insight on by doing this process? Write down your intent on a blank page in your journal with the date and time.

Take yourself to your chosen space and make yourself comfortable and meditate or enter into a reflective state. The key is not to push the mind to seek solutions but to let it completely relax into the awareness that pervades everything. So just be in the space. Be a witness. Observe the signs in nature around you.

If you allow yourself to gently immerse yourself in the pure awareness that you can instinctively feel underneath all phenomena, you will become aware of how the natural world reflects the nature of your issues back to you. From these observations, spontaneous solutions and ideas will arise.

Journal anything significant that comes, even if, at this stage, it seems insignificant or you've yet to fully understand its meaning. You can use the exercises in the next two chapters to explore any signs, symbols or characteristics of any wildlife that visited you during your quest.

We're all connected to everything. Acknowledge this at the end of your retreat by putting your hands on the Earth and simply thanking the space for its insights and wisdom.

Knowing Yourself

We could, of course, just leave our dreams well alone. They would go on reorganizing us without our conscious interference. Is there any benefit to be had by analysing or interpreting them? I would argue there is. What of recurring dreams, for instance? Do you think the miracle of a machine that you inhabit would need to keep having the same dream, like a stuck record? Don't you think it would be able to sort the problem out the first time round? It's a sign of imbalance or dysfunction at some level. To resolve it, the unconscious needs the assistance of the conscious mind, so it keeps flagging up the helpline number, hoping we'll take notice. In my experience of working with people's dreams, once a recurring dream is consciously explored and its meanings realized, it disappears. Balance is once more restored.

We seek to control things in our day-to-day lives because we are seeking certainty in our world. Certainty makes us feel safe; it makes us feel able to carry on, to be able to cope. Otherwise the world is too big and scary. Having more understanding and communication with your unconscious mind allows you to exert more control and therefore have more certainty over your world. You'll have more experience available to you and more access to information.

It feels comfortable to truly know ourselves. We tend to be more accepting of who we are. We come to understand our own individuality and that of others. We are less judgemental. We feel happier, more at peace, balanced and calm.

The Story We Tell Ourselves

Let's take a moment to explore how we make up our perceptions of the world with a simple example. A coffee lover comes into contact with coffee through the sense door of the nose, i.e. smells it. The aroma instantly triggers all the feelings that person associates with coffee, which have built up over time through their association with the object – all those moments of relaxation with friends, getting going in the morning and good conversations over late-night dinners. This happens in a split second and leads to their immediate perception of coffee as a good thing. 'It makes me feel that I

belong.' 'It aids my creativity.' 'It wakes me up.' This leads
to the action of having a cup of coffee to satisfy the feelings
elicited. Of course, we all have different perceptions, so
if you dislike coffee your reaction would be the opposite.
And rarely does the habit deliver the goods, because it's not
the real issue. What we really want is to fulfil our deeper
sense of loneliness and wanting to relax. To break free from
these habitual loops of entanglement, learn to pause before
activating the habit and ask, 'For what purpose?' For example,
'For what purpose am I smoking this cigarette?' 'To relax, to
have five minutes to myself' may be the answer. What you
really want then is not the cigarette but what's underneath the
cigarette, which is to relax and take five minutes. This is the
same for all habits. It is not the habit but what we perceive the
habit gives us that we're really seeking. Once we understand
this we can find more positive ways to give ourselves what
we really want. Dreams always helpfully highlight our faulty
reasoning and perceptions.

Believing is Seeing

We are all actually experiencing the world via our nervous
system. No external representation actually exists. This is fact.
Our eyes do not see what we think they see. They're actually
receiving a constant influx of tiny electrical impulses which
they convert into pictures imprinted upside down on a screen
at the back of our head.

In fact the 'I'll believe it when I see it' saying that we're so
indoctrinated with in the Western rational world is actually the
wrong way round. The truth is, 'We'll see it when we believe
it.' We get what we believe. Every single cell of our body is
eavesdropping on our internal representations. If we work on
being in communication with these we effect instantaneous
change simply through shifting our perception. So, though we
may not be able to change an event, we can always change
the internal representation of it by changing our perception or
point of view – and then change *can* happen.

The external life events we witness are simply a result of our communication with our unconscious mind. As Jung said, 'People marry their unconscious mind.'

Dreams are a brilliant way of shifting our point of view to one more accurately in line with who we truly are. If we translate a dream and it changes our perception about an issue, that's it, job done. The realization and shift of perception change the external forever.

We've all had experiences of this. If you've ever been in relationship with somebody you dearly loved and you're no longer with them, at some point your perception of that person changed, and once changed it was impossible to go back to that original feeling, wasn't it? You could no longer see them in the same light. That shift of opinion had the power to change your life. Change your mind, change your destiny. It really is that simple. Not always easy to do, but certainly simple.

Dreams help us in this process by highlighting issues for us to look at or explore. Our true beliefs show up in our dreams. In my dream experience it has become apparent that our most intense dreams or periods of dreaming are always relevant to our current conscious life events in some form or manner. They are absolutely irretrievably linked.

A funny example of this was a dream I had whilst writing this book. Part of my research was to locate certain dreams from well-known personalities. I dreamed that I was flying a giant dream-catching spaceship. I was navigating across the universe, hunting down dreams. On waking I realized that perfectly summed up the enormity of the task I'd set myself in the time available!

Building Good Communication between our Minds

Because the unconscious mind holds such a vast store of data it needs to find a way of allowing us to access large chunks in a relatively easy manner. 'A picture tells a thousand words' is a statement we all know and understand, and its relevance to dreams and our unconscious is obvious. A sequence of events in a dream is, in reality, a complex multi-layered communication between the unconscious and conscious minds. Every detail is relevant. The more you become accustomed to working with your dreams, the more you'll discover this to be true. It is easy to work with dreams and learn more about yourself – all you have to do is follow the suggestions and exercises outlined in this book and soon, with a bit of practice, you too will be a master of dream appreciation.

We get our minds talking to each other by trusting the information we receive. We tend to dismiss the messages of our unconscious mind because they're presented in inexplicable ways, ways that we don't immediately understand. So we need to build trust in the unconscious. We can start to do this by choosing to tell ourselves a different story. Separate the facts of a situation from your perception of it, the story you're telling yourself about the reality you perceive. Or, as Richard Bandler put it, 'It's never too late to have a happy childhood.' As adults we become too conditioned to other people's ideas of right and wrong rather than forming opinions from our own continued experiential learning and developing wisdom.

TOP TIP

To build trust in your intuitive self, pause during the day and state three words about how you're feeling at that moment, for example, 'Tired, happy, curious.' Don't think about it, just come out with them.

This starts to get you in tune with where you're at. It helps you to begin to pay attention to the thoughts that are going on in your head. Remember, 'As a man thinketh, so he becomes.'

Also, pay attention to your dreams, intuition and hunches – the more you prove yourself right by following your instincts and getting a positive result, the more you'll be encouraged to continue. In this way your life will begin to change for the better naturally.

This is not about the destination, it really is about enjoying the journey. There's no end point with dreams. The unconscious hosts a vast awareness with infinite possibilities. Dreams are your intimate companions, your new best friends, filled with helpful tips, excellent advice, warnings or fun and games. They love you enough to tell you off or call you on your stuff when necessary. They'll be there to the end, supporting and encouraging you all the way, but your conscious mind has to act on that advice to make it manifest, otherwise it stays just a dream.

Once you've worked on a couple of dreams using the exercises in Chapters Five and Six, you'll be able to know your dreams more easily. Erstwhile nonsense will become startling clear. I've seen this happen countless times in dream groups and workshops. A dream makes absolutely no sense to someone, then, using one of the many simple translation techniques given throughout this book, suddenly they understand it and can see the personal wisdom inherent in it. Just one experience of that is normally enough to make a dream convert of anyone. It's a heady feeling to clearly understand a dream. There's a sense of wonderment in it.

Most of us get to know the unconscious mind gradually, in stages. Through meditation, contemplation and moments of awe in life we get glimpses of its perfection and infinite nature. This bliss state appears more frequently the more we give ourselves permission to explore our inner world and its cornucopia of riches. But the unconscious also communicates with us on a more mundane, prosaic level in our daily concerns and can show us those less savoury aspects of ourselves we don't wish to admit to. We'll always find our thoughts reflected in our external world if we know how to perceive them and are honest enough with ourselves to admit the truth, however unpalatable that may be at times.

Self-Responsibility

Of course, realizing the power inherent in our dreaming mind brings with it a need to take responsibility for our thoughts, words and actions. This is what many of us shy away from. Better to live in ignorance and accept fate than have to own up to the fact that we're responsible for co-creating our reality – especially when that reality is less than ideal.

But if you want to live a powerful, fulfilling, happy life, be at cause not effect. Be responsible for every aspect of your life. You may not be able to change the facts, but you always have the choice to change your perception of them and can choose how to respond to them. That will create new perspectives around familiar terrain and that is the key to all change. You only need look to your dreaming mind; it's the perfect feedback loop for running your own extraordinarily successful Me, Inc.

I disagree with the premise that we're broken and need fixing in some way. I believe we're all magnificent and perfect already. We may, though, have adopted some unhelpful behaviour patterns, limiting beliefs and negative emotions along the way. These become layered on top of our perfection and these layers can stop us achieving our dreams.

Our unconscious, however, is a great friend and the Dream Whisperer will reveal our true magnificence to us. So, engaging with our dreams isn't about over-analysing ourselves and thinking, 'Oh God, I really messed up, I'm never going to recover.' It's about 'Wow, that's really interesting. I didn't realize I thought that.' It's a more positive process. It's about realizing we're already perfect but sometimes we need to peel off a few layers to reveal that perfection.

One of my students recently asked me why, if human beings were so perfect, dreams were so challenging and difficult to understand. First, I don't agree they *are* difficult to understand – we just need the right tools and then they reveal themselves very quickly, simply and clearly, as you'll soon discover. The unconscious has to use symbolic representations for speed and efficiency. If it delivered insights in a linear fashion, it would be too much for our conscious mind to take. Thinking back to our global corporation, our Me, Inc., there would be reams of management reports to wade through, which, to my mind, is not half as much fun as a good juicy dream!

There's another reason too. Dreams reveal our inner truth, and true self-expression requires us to be vulnerable. In order to make ourselves vulnerable, we need to feel safe. Dreams are a safety valve, one that we have the key to unlock. If they were easy to understand, everyone would be able to see the inner workings of our psyche (if we told them about our dreams, of course) and we would feel too exposed.

The point is that reality is always our *perceptual* reality. Which is great, because it means we can shift and change it, and the more we understand this, the more we can change it for the better. Remember you're the boss of Me, Inc. You're in charge. Now where do you want your dreams to take you?

CHAPTER FIVE

Symbol and Metaphor

Creating your own Dream Bible

'A dream which is not interpreted is like a letter which is not opened.'
The Talmud

All good treasure maps are full of symbolic clues, intriguing hieroglyphs and indecipherable code to protect the treasure from being discovered by those for whom it was not meant. So are your dreams. They have meanings hidden in a code decipherable only by you. Luckily, help is at hand to break those codes. Our own dreams are perfectly comprehensible if we understand symbol and metaphor. But before we begin analysing our symbols, a word about creating a dream dictionary.

A Dream Dictionary

The best dream dictionary will always be our own, compiled from the ongoing interpretation of our individual dreams. That's why I want you to begin yours now. The sooner you start, the quicker it will build into an invaluable source of inner knowledge. As you practise the exercises in this chapter you'll be collecting entries for your dictionary. However, it is useful, whilst building your dream repertoire, to have at least one reference book as a starting point, a memory jog if you like, that will spark your own ideas about what a particular symbol means.

A very useful dream dictionary, simply because it contains so much in one volume, is *The Element Encyclopaedia of 20,000 Dreams*, by Theresa Cheung. Not because I think it will give you the answer to your specific dream, but if you're not used to working in a metaphorical or symbolic manner, then it's a useful starting point for getting ideas about what you need to think about. Ultimately, though, if, say, a cat turns up in a dream, it's always going to be your specific cat, the cat from your childhood, the cat that you grew up with, your pet. There will be common elements that relate to the general genre of 'cat', but how they relate to the specificity of your dream cat is what you need to be paying attention to.

In terms of creating your dream dictionary, you have two basic options: either create a second written journal that you transcribe symbols from your dreams into, together with their personal meanings and insights or, preferably, in terms of sequencing and search convenience, type your symbols and insights into your PC.

Dream Language

Let's begin with words. Language itself is symbolic. A word cannot ever capture the entirety of an object – it is a useful label only. However, we become conditioned by the world of words, trapped inside it so that we lose our ability to truly perceive what an individual object is. This is vital to understand when working with the unconscious mind, especially at the physical level. To give an example, a client recently suffered from a trigeminal nerve pain in her face. Her entire conversation was peppered with the comment that life 'really gets on my nerves'. Practise paying attention to your friends' and colleagues' language and you'll soon start to hear their symbolic language and personal metaphors reflecting their internal issues.

We're only able to make sense of our realities and communicate with each other using symbols. Language is our symbolic map of the world that allows us to navigate familiar terrain. Of course, this only works when we share a common language and meaning of words. I have had this beautifully illustrated to me by my American family. My father is American but I was brought up in England and it is only in recent years that I have met and begun to develop a relationship with various members of my American family. When I first met my sisters and we were chatting away getting to know each other I noticed my father kept translating what I was saying for them (I'd known him longer and he was better travelled). Although I thought we spoke the same language, they had different meanings or at times no meaning for many of the everyday words I was using, so for them my conversation was, at times, confusing and incomprehensible.

Often dreams use jokes, puns, phrases, key words, songs and other symbolic language devices to convey meaning. Check the language in your dreams. Are there jokes? Does something have an innuendo, a double meaning? Could it be taken another way?

I dreamed a flock of white birds came out and I was told they were terns, because they were rather large...

In this dream, the dreamer was at a major *turning* point in her life – the real meaning of the large terns.

To take another example, once I dreamed of Clarins body products in an upstairs bathroom when asking for clarity.

In dreams, upstairs in a house usually refers to the future or the Higher Self, and water, via the shower, is representative of cleansing emotions and memories. So my dream meant my clarity would come from connecting to my Higher Self through the emotional cleansing of past memories. Suddenly a dreaming pun has depth of meaning and real relevance to life.

Here's a great exercise for unlocking your symbolic words, jokes and puns and the meanings behind them:

SYMBOLIC DREAM WORDS

Underline all the key symbols or words in your dream. Take each in turn and ask the following questions of it. Do it quickly and write the first things that come to mind.

* What is the purpose of X for me?

* What does X mean to me?

* What is the function of X?

* What else could X mean?

* What does X remind me of?

* How does X make me feel?

* How does X relate to my current life?

And always to end:

* And what do I know now?

This exercise begins to loosen your thinking around the dream and tap into your unconscious knowledge of the symbols and words involved. Look at the answers you have written and you will start to find recurring themes and patterns. This exercise alone may immediately solve the meaning of the dream for you.

What is the Best Way to Understand the Symbolic Language of our Dreams?

Imagery is our primary processing system and language our second. Symbols are generally closer to images, so we can see or imagine a symbol without always being able to describe it fully in words. Once an experience has evolved into a symbol (an object), it can be picked up and carried across the dreaming bridge to our conscious awareness. So work with the information you get, not that which you can verbalize.

This is about building a subjective synthesis, a personal search engine that will allow you to make connections, see patterns and retrieve information with which to reveal the meaning of your dreams. In dreams your tree will be different from my tree. It will mean something entirely different to you than it does to me. Nevertheless, understanding the symbolism of the tree genre will point you in the right direction. For example, trees are generally seen as symbols of longevity, wisdom, family relationships (the family tree), deep roots, tradition, conservatism and strength. Within our two dreams on trees, we would start looking at those different areas represented by the generic tree symbol. However, that's where the common thread would end. Your dream tree might be to do with your grandfather being about to die or with severing family roots, and mine might be to do with the fact that I had a row with my sister last week or I'm struggling with buying a new house, putting down my roots. Our interpretations would be very different, but knowing about trees would help us know where to start the search. That's why building up our search engine knowledge is so useful.

A basic understanding of directions, colours and numerology helps build our dream-interpretation search engine and you'll find these attributes listed in the Appendix on page 249.

Numbers are a primary structure in our lives and they occur regularly in dreams in many different forms. It's always worth noticing what numbers show up. Let's take an example to illustrate the power of a little appropriate knowledge;

In your dream you notice that it's 2.15 a.m. This seems very significant and it is a clear detail that stays with you when you wake. With a basic understanding of numbers, you would know two is about relationships and union, one is about individuality and five is about conflict and transformation. Is this dream actually indicating the need for a current relationship to transform or end? Are you missing your independence? Or are you commitment phobic and need to explore transforming your independence into an ability to share intimacy with others? Look at the calendar significance of those numbers, 15 February. Is that a significant birthday or date in your life? Does that relate to a special anniversary of some kind? Suddenly we have a lot of meaningful information to explore way beyond 'Oh, it's 2.15 in my dream.'

Interpreting Symbols

Based on the ideas of Freud, this next exercise will go far in unlocking the meaning of your personal dream words and symbols. It wakes your brain up to seeing the connections and when done in a meditative state it connects you with your dreaming mind. Rather than write a list, I think using mind maps yields better results, as they keep us connected to our intuitive dreamy right side of the brain.

FREE ASSOCIATION EXERCISE

The key to the success of this technique is to relax and write down whatever comes into your brain. Let go of your self-judgement and preconceptions. Adopt a Zen beginner's mind approach each time you use the exercise. Trust your unconscious mind to know the answers and give yourself a chance to hear them. As soon as you start thinking, 'This is silly. What a dumb idea. Why am I doing this?' forget it, take a break and come back to it later, as you'll have lost the flow.

Take any dream you wish to work with and go through it and list all its separate symbolic components, for example, 'a bridge', 'a scary man', 'a tidal wave', etc., each on a separate piece of paper. Have more spare paper ready for doing the exercise.

You can use this exercise to work on as many or as few symbols in a dream as you wish. If pushed for time, choose four symbols that shout at you from the dream. Perhaps a gnarled tree, an old house or a huge spider – they're all symbols. Use your intuition. You'll spend your whole life doing dream interpretation if you don't get good at using your intuition. Pick the symbols that stick out or you think seem weird or odd or that repeat themselves. Look for the ones that are calling your attention.

It's best if you choose a recent dream or a long-standing recurring dream because obviously it's going to have more relevance to what's currently going on in your life. Write each of the four down in the centre of a separate piece of paper.

You can do this for a person, a colour or an object. The only thing you can't really do this for is dream feelings. This exercise is about revealing the encoded message in the symbols rather than the feelings.

Now let's begin...

Uncross your legs and close your eyes, take a deep breath, bring your awareness into your belly and ... take some slow, deep, quiet, long breaths in through the nose and out through the nose, becoming aware of the space around your skin... Tune into the stillness of the physical space you're in and ... with each exhale just allow yourself to let go a little more, to sink into yourself, and just relax deeper and deeper and deeper...

Imagine the crown of your head opening and a beautiful white light just like rain pouring down through your open crown and washing through your brain, and as that white light washes through your brain, your brain becomes empty and clear as the light simply washes all the words and thoughts away ... all the way, away now ... so the words and thoughts just drip through your brain, down through your arms and drip into the floor through the ends of your fingers and toes. The beautiful white shower of light is cleansing, purifying you, clearing you of the need to think, softening your mind, letting it go for a moment. Just relax and let the white light clear the screen of your mind, the screen of thoughts just washed away. See a giant set of windscreen wipers and as a thought comes in it just gets wiped away through the white light of rain. That's right ... very good.

And in that calm, relaxed state, gently open your eyes, pick up your paper and write the first symbol in a circle in the middle. Now mind map your associations with this symbol. Write down everything connected with it, not censoring your words, letting go and letting them flow. Each new thought will lead to another thought. Follow the chain of thought. Follow a thought as if it's on a piece of string. Tug at it until you can bring it close enough to quite literally hear it whispering to you. Keep going until there is nothing left, you simply run out of steam. Then move on to the next symbol. (For an example, see my six minute mind map, opposite.)

If you want to take a different sheet of paper for each symbol, do so. If you find you're thinking, you're not doing it. Relax again and move on. Move quickly through the list of symbols until you've finished.

Now review your list. Notice, underline, mark any common themes or patterns that have emerged. Make a note of any relationships that you can see between any combination of the associations that you've written.

Six Minute Mind Map

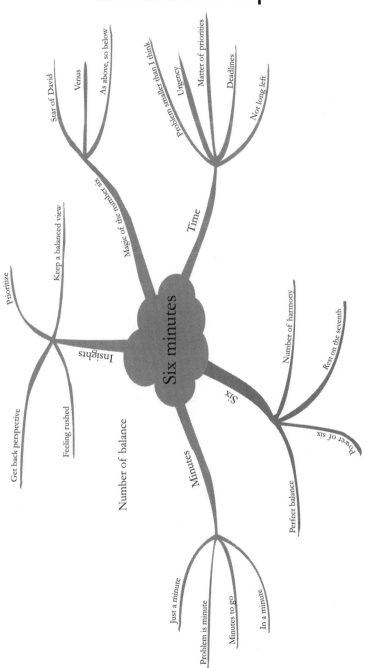

Here's an example from a dream workshop to illustrate the process:

I dream about the sea quite a bit. This time the sea was dirty, full of silt. There was a string of large cardboard boxes going right out into it. All the boxes were attached by a string and I got on one box and ran along quite easily to the furthest box. My daughter was coming behind me and she was having problems. My husband was on the shore and he hadn't made it.

At the time of the dream my daughter was very ill with depression. What surprised me was one of the words I put down for the sea was 'outcast', which was unusual for me, because all the other things I put down were emotions. Some of the matching words were for cardboard boxes – 'soft' and 'easily damaged' – and for the string I had 'soft', 'weak' and 'lost'.

Clearly 'outcast' is the active word here. Interestingly, cardboard boxes are also what is 'cast out' after we have taken out what's inside the package. I wonder what aspect of the dreamer is feeling like an outcast? The ocean refers to our emotions and memories. Perhaps this dreamer feels emotionally outcast because she is unable to reach her daughter in her depression.

Immediately we can begin to see how useful this quick and easy tool is. This is one of the first things to do with any dream, once we've pondered it as a whole for a while and free associated or mind mapped anything that immediately springs to mind. Simply underline the components, free associate and let your dream meanings reveal themselves. This specificity begins to build our personal dream dictionaries. Many people dream about the ocean, for example, but remember your ocean is different from my ocean. Your ocean could be from a holiday that you went on last year, whilst mine might be from when I nearly drowned as a child.

The Me, Me, Me of Dream Interpretation

Always relate your dream content back to yourself, however strange that content might seem. Take a dream symbol and think, 'What does this mean to me?' Then apply what you discover to your own life. For example, if you get birds in your dreams, remember that birds are often about messages from the Higher Self. Look to your life and think, 'What messages am I being given in my life? Well, I just got this contract through and I've got this idea for a new job, so maybe I need to be looking at that.' Then question yourself further: 'What were the birds doing in the dream? They were aggressively attacking me. Maybe this contract isn't the right one for me right now.' This is the process we're engaging with. This is what gives the dream its power.

Another way of working with Me, Inc. and symbols is simply to write out your dream and each time you reach a symbol, write 'aspect of me' after it. Here's an example to illustrate:

I'm on a platform (aspect of me). I'm waiting for a Circle Line tube (aspect of me). The platform (aspect of me) is only two carriages (aspect of me) long, so when the train (aspect of me) comes along it's got to park itself precisely in order for me to get on it

This technique alone can reveal some surprising insights and it reminds you to keep focused on how the dream relates to you.

You can sometimes have a dream that seems quite normal and there'll be one element that sticks out or seems completely random. Work on that element. Always work on what really stands out, 'speaks to you' in some way or seems most peculiar. That will often be the clue or the key that unlocks the rest of the dream. Also look for what repeats or is exaggerated in the dream.

Below is a dream technique I developed from the emergence work I did with the late David Grove and subsequently through the Emergence Practice Group facilitated by Deborah Henley. It works really well for dreams that seem to elude more obvious interpretation techniques.

PUZZLING DREAMS

Take a dream that is puzzling you, one that you just know is important but whose meaning you can't quite grasp. Have your journal or a notebook ready.

Draw something on a piece of paper that symbolically represents the dream. Make it as simple or elaborate as you wish, but ensure that you relate the dream to the image you draw.

Imagine the room you're working in represents your life and place this dream symbol physically somewhere in the room that feels right to you and position yourself in the right place in relation to it.

You can check you've set it up correctly by asking yourself the following questions:

✳ Am I in the right place in relation to my dream?

✳ Am I at the right distance from my dream?

Also ask the dream picture:

✳ Is my dream in the right place?

✳ Is my dream at the right distance from me? (You might also like to consider whether its height and angle are right for you.)

Make whatever adjustments you need to as a result of these questions and repeat the questions until both you and your dream are in the right place.

It is important that you *write* down your answers to the following questions, as this serves to pause your thinking and allows the answers to become clear to you. Ask yourself:

✳ And what do I know about my dream from my current perspective?

✳ Is there anything else I know from this space here?

✳ From my dream's perspective what does my dream know?

✳ Is there anything else my dream knows from this space here?

✳ And from the perspective of the space, what does the space between me and my dream know?

✳ Is there anything else the space between me and my dream knows?

Write down everything. Don't judge or limit your response.

You may like to continue by asking yourself if there is another space the dream could move to and repeat the above process from this new space. You can do this up to six times. There is magic in the number six.

Always end the process with the following questions to ensure your insights relate back to your current life and reality:

✳ And what do I know now?

✳ And is there anything else I know now?

Keep repeating this question to yourself until you are empty – you've run out of words.

End with the following questions to complete the process:

✳ What insights did I discover?

✳ What difference has that made?

✳ What action do I need to take as a result of this new information?

✳ What would I like to have happen now?

✳ What do I expect will happen now?

Remember that ultimately the meaning of anything is made up. Which is why a dream can only be fully understood by the dreamer, because they're the one making it up, so they're the one it will make sense to. Others can certainly facilitate understanding, however, as I do with clients.

Sliding Up and Down the Dream Scale

We need to develop flexibility in unlocking symbols. This assists us in eliciting helpful meaning. This next technique is designed to do exactly that. You can use it with any dream aspect to get a broader context if it's a specific item or a specific context if it's a general dream theme.

If we have something very specific in our dream, for example, a purple car, it helps to slide up the dream scale to elicit its higher purpose by asking the following questions:

✳ What's the purpose of the purple car? *To transport me from A to B.*
✳ What's the purpose of transport? *To move something from one location to another.*
✳ What's the purpose of moving something from one location to another? *To make progress.*
✳ What's the intention of making progress? *To grow and develop.*

And so on until you can go no further.
Other useful questions to ask are:

✳ What's the intention of X?
✳ What does X do for me?
✳ How does X serve me?
✳ What is X an example of?

In this way we begin to see that our purple car actually relates to growth, development and progress in our life.

If we experience something very general in our dreams, for example a dark shadow, then we need to slide down the dream scale to discover its specific meaning for us by asking the following questions:

✳ What specifically is that dark shadow? *It's an unnamed fear, something I'm hiding from.*
✳ What specifically is that unnamed fear I'm hiding from? *I'm scared that we're going to lose our home.*
✳ What specifically is it about losing my home I'm scared of? *That my marriage won't survive the emotional upheaval.*

And so on until you're really clear on what the issue is.

Suddenly a dark shadow is revealed to be a fear of losing a marriage which, now it is understood, can be dealt with. That's the power of your dreams!

Other useful questions to ask are:

✳ What are other examples of X?
✳ What kind of X is that?

This exercise is worth doing with all dreams, as it allows you to slide up to find the higher purpose of your dream and to slide back down to understand how that higher purpose relates to your current life situation. It works because it follows the basic underpinning structure of our physical existence: the expansion and contraction of energy.

If you've discovered a course of action is being suggested by your dream, ask yourself the following reality-check questions:

✳ On a scale of 1–10, where 1 is not taking action and 10 is solving the problem, how certain am I that I'll take the necessary action? (Record the first number that comes into your head – don't think about it.)

✳ If less than 10, what would make it a 10?
✳ If I don't change this/do this, what will it mean?
✳ If I don't change this/do this, what will it cost me?
✳ Why do I want this?
✳ What limiting belief, bad habit or negative emotion has been preventing me from living the life of my dreams?

Dream Metaphors

We speak in metaphors all the time and so do our dreams. It's unpacking them that gets us clear on what's happening. By working with our dreams, we learn about ourselves and can change what we don't like and maintain and improve what we do. Change does require a context, though, and the metaphor of the dream is the context. Metaphors allow us to understand ourselves and the system we inhabit. In the previous chapter, I used the metaphor of Me, Inc. and the interaction between boss and employees to help us to better understand the relationship between the conscious and unconscious minds.

We ourselves are a whole system and we need to utilize whole-system thinking in order to resolve our issues. Within a problem, there are symptoms. It is a problem because the symptoms have not yet resolved themselves. We have within ourselves all we need to heal, yet our system is so vast our conscious mind can't possibly be aware of all the resources we have to solve the problem. Listening to and working with our dreams allow us to access that curative element within our system, because these symptoms turn up in our dreams as symbols. We need to interrogate our dream symbols and metaphors until they reveal their wisdom to us.

In dream work, we're not attempting to solve the symptoms of the dream. We want to honour the symptom and allow it to achieve its aim. It has purpose and the ability to heal inherent within it. We want to work with the symbols and metaphors, as they're containers of information, personal gifts containing all we need to grow, develop and be the shining souls we are.

Through this process, change occurs naturally. It doesn't need to be forced; it happens as our understanding changes. In other words, the whole system changes itself by new information becoming available. In metaphysical understanding we're all aspects of the universe experiencing itself. This is the same process that occurs in our dreaming mind. It is the feedback loop of our entire experience.

In dream work, you'll notice many changes take place as you work through the exercises in this book. Some of them will occur without your conscious awareness of them and some you need to bring to conscious understanding. Back at Me, Inc., mostly the employees can take responsibility for the day-to-day running of the business and make necessary adjustments without constantly checking in with the boss. The boss sees the results, so knows the work is being done. On other occasions, the boss has to get involved because the workforce needs their active engagement to solve whatever issue has cropped up.

Let's illustrate this with a couple of metaphoric dreams, the first from Dr David Shephard, Certified Master Trainer of NLP, Time Line Therapy and Hypnosis:

I was having a drink in the pub with friends, a traditional old London pub with a large circular bar in the centre. I had an old gentleman's walking cane. It was black with a silver knob on top. This was a cane with a difference. If you pointed it across the room, it would float across the room and stick to the wall on the other side.

I was playing with the cane in the pub and one of my friends asked if he could have a go. I agreed. He pointed it at the ceiling above the middle of the circular bar and let go. It floated across the room and fixed itself to the high ceiling in the middle of the bar where I couldn't reach it. I was annoyed.

I fell asleep in the pub and when I awoke all my friends were gone. I left the pub and could see them walking up the hill outside. I followed them. I caught them up just as they reached the top of the hill. One of them spotted me and invited me to join them for dinner. I turned them down, saying that if they had wanted me to join them for dinner they'd have woken me up.

I walked back to the pub. I wanted my cane back. I stood at the bar, but I couldn't reach the cane. I knew that the only way I could get my cane back was to ask someone behind the bar. I was incredibly uncomfortable about doing that, yet I knew it was the only way for me to get my cane. The more I thought about it, the stronger the feeling got until it woke me up.

And here's David's interpretation of his dream metaphor:

The circular bar is the circle used in magic. The cane represented a magical 'technique'. At this time, I was developing magically with a group of friends. I understood that there was a magical technique that I needed/wanted and I would get it on my own rather than with my friends. I would have to ask someone for it and I would know the person but I would be very uncomfortable asking them for it and if I were to get it I would have to forego that uncomfortable feeling and ask. I knew immediately who it was and as soon as I thought of asking him I got the same uncomfortable feeling. But I knew I had to ask, so I did. He said that he had been waiting for me to ask and then gave me a very secret and ancient Sanskrit chant.

So a powerful learning and resolution were uncovered from the dream story.

The next dreamer's epic illustrates wonderfully the symbolic and metaphoric story of dreams. A 47-year-old married woman with children who works as a coach in leadership development, she has in recent years begun to develop a deeper shamanic practice, travelling to Peru and undertaking vision quests. The shift this spiritual unfolding is creating in her psyche is reflected in the symbolism of this dream:

I am in the forest with a bunch of people. We're standing behind a white canvas fence put up in a circle among the trees. The fence surrounds us. A snow leopard appears in front of me on the other side of the fence. She is big and looks like a female lion – white with the pattern of a leopard. She looks right at me and gets ready to jump. I draw away from the fence. She jumps and some of the other people put down the white canvas fence, so she jumps into the circle and lies down right in front of me. I am surprised that she has been able to jump over and into the circle. She lies down on her stomach, alert. I stand in front of her and say a prayer: 'Thank you, dear friend, for coming to visit us and for hunting in the forest.' I am afraid, but pretend, in a queen-like fashion, to be used to having a snow leopard pay me a visit! I want her to leave, so I say something in order to make her decide just that.

We can see that this dream reflects the dreamer's need to conquer her fears and connect to her truth. The snow leopard is a metaphor for the opportunity and gift of power to conquer one's demons with great energy and vitality. The white circle fence is symbolic of protection. The snow leopard is a rare and secretive beast – to have one visit you, even in a dream, is a precious gift indeed! Snow leopards represent intuitive powers and the ability to take great leaps in life. They inhabit high mountainous regions, so there is a symbolic link here with the dreamer connecting to her spirit and inner wisdom (often represented by mountains). This is particularly relevant for this woman, as the spiritual practices of Peru involve acknowledgement of the mountain spirits as a source of wisdom and she is of an age where metaphysically she would be considered to be entering her wisdom years.

A great way of working with a dream like this would
be to do a meditative journey when awake to reconnect
with the snow leopard and resolve the metaphor positively,
thereby healing the issues within your unconscious mind
on an energetic level. There are plenty of journey exercises
within this book to help you with dreams such as this. Use
the following questions within the meditation to assist you in
making the metaphor work:

* What's not working for me in the dream?
* What do I want instead?
* What prevents me from having what I want?
* How is that a problem?
* What's of interest or value to me?
* What's important to me?
* What would be the perfect metaphor to work with to
  resolve this dream? (Allow the dream images to reform
  into a new metaphor that works for you.)
* And what can happen now?
* And what action would I like to take to honour that new
  understanding?

If we take the snow leopard dream as an example, this could
be revisited as a shamanic initiation metaphor where the
dreamer shapeshifts and merges with the energy of the snow
leopard and travels with the beast to new pastures, safe under
the tutelage of this powerful totem animal but free of the
constricting boundaries of the overprotective white fence.

You'll know whether you're interpreting your dream
messages correctly when you get that 'Aha!' feeling. It creates
a distinct, albeit subtle, physiological shift in the body. You
may feel a lightness or sensation of expansiveness or perhaps
feel very warm. Or you may feel something else that is unique
to you, but you will know. You'll absolutely know inside that
it's right.

Now it's time to get better acquainted with our nightly visitors – those strange men, women and beasts that constantly populate our dreams with agendas and antics that we need to understand.

CHAPTER SIX

Universal Energy

The Role of Archetypes and Myth

'The dream is an invaluable commentator and illuminator of life. Listen to the wisdom of the dream.'
Carl Jung

Dreams have layers of information available to work from: the personal unconscious, the collective unconscious and the daily conscious. These tend to work in unison and most dreams have multi-layered levels of meaning. Rarely is there such a thing as a purely symbolic, day-residue or personal unconscious dream; mostly, they are a combination of all three. We'll certainly always encounter unresolved personal stuff and that can be reflected in our dream via the archetypal images of what Jung termed the 'collective unconscious', the collective myth we're universally steeped in. In this chapter we're going to focus further on the language of dreams by investigating these archetypes.

What Are Archetypes?

Archetypes are universal energy experiences that cross cultures, gender and age. They're often personified as iconic figures that symbolize a multitude of universally recognizable energies. They turn up in our dreams to convey larger messages about our existence that ordinary information cannot convey. We need to understand the aspects of ourselves these characters represent in order to know ourselves better.

Archetypes are everywhere – in movies, fairy tales, company logos, art, fashion, jewellery and advertising. There are individual and universal archetypes. We become aware of our personal archetypes during dreamtime, journeying and meditation. They typically, but not exclusively, turn up as characters in our dreams. Many of them we're already familiar with. Most of us will have a mother and father figure appearing in our dreams, for example. Jung also talks about the anima and the animus. These are the characters that symbolize our opposite sexual energies, though we all contain both feminine and masculine aspects. There will always be a shadow archetype as well, a character, symbol or beast that represents our darker psyche, that part of ourselves that we don't always want to admit the presence of. That scary monster, that person that you don't really want to face, is just a part of ourselves that we're not prepared to look at. If we do start to look at these scary aspects, we get a huge amount of information about who we are, what we're doing and why. Armed with that information, we can make changes in our behaviour or attitudes that will help us.

In our dreamtime we'll encounter certain archetypes more often than others. These normally represent those deeper patterns that we habitually repeat, the recurring themes and elements of our dreams and lives. The more we record and review our dreams, the easier these patterns are to see. Suddenly we have a road map of where we're heading and what direction we need to be taking, what issues we need to be focusing on and how to resolve them. If we're being chased by a dark unknown assailant who terrifies us, for example, we need to reveal that aspect to ourselves, confront the inner demon and grow. Unknown people in our dreams represent unknown parts of ourselves, i.e. our unconscious, whereas people we know in dreams tend to represent collective opinions that we've assimilated or aspects of the self characterized by what those people mean to us.

Using Tarot Cards for Dream Work

Jung created his idea of archetypes from his knowledge of the Major Arcana of the Tarot. Myers Briggs, creator of the popular personality-profiling tool, also uses Jung's Tarot symbolism very effectively in his work. Only the 22 Major Arcana cards are used because these represent the mythical hero's journey outlined in Joseph Campbell's *The Hero with a Thousand Faces*. It's the cyclical story of everyone's life. To paraphrase: we're born innocent, we meet our heavenly parents, our earthly parents, our church and our community. We undergo our rites of passage, we're initiated, we leave home, embark on a quest, suffer the long dark night of the soul, find our mentors, get help, fight and conquer the evil demons, find the saviours and eventually stand up to be judged and return home into enlightenment. We continuously run through cycles of this hero's journey throughout our life, through every kind of phase of life that we go through. Learning to walk is part of the hero's journey. We go from sitting to crawling to standing to walking through many obstacles, falls and encouragement along the way.

An excellent way to familiarize yourself with the basic archetypes of your life journey is to buy a Rider Waite Tarot deck and do the following exercise. (You could use another deck, too, but in my opinion the Rider Waite is second to none in terms of its esoteric symbolism and it's the absolute best at depicting the hero's journey.)

ARCHETYPE FIRST IMPRESSIONS

Take out the 22 Major Arcana cards from the deck you've chosen and keep them with your dream journal.

Choose a dream you'd like to work on.

Shuffle the cards whilst keeping the dream in mind and ask them to show you what universal or archetypal energy this dream is illustrating.

Use your non-dominant hand to pick a card randomly from the pack. Record the name of the archetype next to your dream. The basic attributes of the cards are listed in the Appendix on page 249, but before turning to these, intuitively sense what the image revealed means to you and how it relates to your dream. Interpretations of archetypes are, like dreams, both universal and personal, so always record your personal impressions first.

Begin also to recognize how the archetypal associations you discover are reflected in your life.

Once you get the measure of how the archetype is showing up in your life, refer back to the dream to see if the energy was positive or negative. That is, how was this character showing up in your dream? Were they exhibiting negative behaviour, illustrating the shadow elements you need to release or harmonize within yourself, or were they showing you the positive attributes of the character that you need to incorporate more of into your life?

Which archetypes are at play, and when, will be unique to you, but you'll notice that when you're undergoing rites of passage – leaving home as a teenager, getting married, giving birth, changing career, undergoing divorce, remarriage or a mid-life crisis, getting old or getting sick, getting close to death – where you have to leave behind something in order to embrace a new way of being, these events tend to produce more archetypal dreams. It's as though you're tapping into the human commonality of that experience. In this sense, they're wisdom dreams. A universal energy is entering your dreamscape to show you what energies you need to adopt or release in order to progress on your personal mythic adventure.

Internationally acclaimed opera singer Sir Willard White experienced this archetypal dream of his immortal spirit recently, as he moved into his wisdom years:

In the dream I was living just beyond the Lincoln Center complex in New York City. The New York Philharmonic's building was there, on a big square. One of the short cuts to my apartment was in front of the New York Philharmonic via a side road, which was defined by a huge wall – no windows, just a huge marble white wall. I would walk by some refurbishing construction work, where I had to cross. People were working on the building and the road outside. I passed this area several times.

On this particular day, I was walking near the wall when all of a sudden it just collapsed. It was happening in such a way that I knew I would not survive. I told myself, 'Oh well, here we go, this is the end, no point running, because if I run it's going to get me anyway, so just get on with it.'

It crushed me, but immediately I was alive again in a different physical form. It was more spiritual but nonetheless still a part of this world and so I went on about my business, somewhat enlightened.

What was interesting to me is that I've had dreams about dying before, but just before the moment of death I would wake up.

Death itself is a common dream archetype and is representative of our personal capacity for metamorphosis, in this case spiritual transformation. Although archetypes can be objects such as the building (archetype of the psyche) in the above dream, they will generally turn up as characters. For example, if your mother appears in a dream, then yes, it may have something to do with your actual mother, but it's more likely to be representative of the archetypal mother energies – that is, your need to be mothered at that time, to feel protected, to feel safe, or, if you have children, perhaps it is about your role as a parent. Look at what the dream is telling you about how you need to behave in relationship to the universal energies of the mother rather than take it literally as referring to your mother.

Discovering your Dream Archetypes

One of the major clues that a dream is about archetypes is being aware of nothing in the dream being from our ordinary reality. Many dreams use what we have a conscious awareness of – what we did yesterday, what we had for tea, etc. That is, the dreaming mind uses what is in our personal unconscious. Sometimes, though, we'll have dreams that seem to come from nothing that we know. These are archetypal dreams coming from the collective unconscious. You can of course have archetypal images within an ordinary dream. They are the image that stands out, that is different – a wild beast, a purple spaceship, a stranger, someone from your distant past, something that is not in your everyday reality, and so on.

There are many archetypes that could show up. You could encounter the wise old man, a mountain, the crone, the virgin, the helper, the nurse, the trickster, a king or queen. You may get the high priestess, representing your intuition, or a demon, which represents your shadow self. In a dream, the shadow archetype could appear as a snake, a monster, a bat, a dark shadow in the corner, night-time, a black ocean or something else of that nature. Your dream is unlikely to be a perfect story of the Big Bad Wolf and Little Red Riding Hood and Grandma in the forest. Your archetypes may present as a flower that represents your enlightened self, or a butterfly reflecting your soul, or the devil representing your shadow – who knows? It is for you to discover your dream archetypes, learn to recognize them and understand what and who they are. Use the exercises in this chapter to discover yours.

Also, always become aware of your position in your dreams. Mostly we play the central role – that's our dream ego, our dream persona if you like, and everything is happening to that dream ego. But occasionally there are dreams where we're outside ourselves, literally watching a dream movie where we don't appear to be in on the action. These dreams show where we're not fully engaged in life. It's important that we're playing the central role, that we are fully engaged within the dream itself.

Gender Issues in Dreamtime

We're all a marriage of opposites. Every one of us has both masculine and feminine energies within us. Jung used the terms *anima* and *animus* to describe this. The anima is the male's feminine aspect and conversely the animus is the woman's masculine counterpart. You are aware of these in action already. We all know men who are very emotionally intelligent and sensitive and women who are more forthright and aggressive. In this context we would say the man was expressing more of his feminine energy and the woman was expressing more of her masculine self.

In men's dreams there will be a female figure representing the feminine aspect of themselves and the opposite male character will appear in women's dreams. So, as a woman you're likely to experience a strong male figure in your dreams. This is not actually a man in your life or an expression of what you feel about men, it's the masculine part of your own self. Similarly, as a man you'll have a strong female archetype in your dreams, which will be the feminine part of yourself that you're not able to express in your conscious daily living. The nature of these characters can change throughout our life.

When we're operating from a good balance between these gender polarities, our dream mates will represent an appropriate balance. Marriage is a good metaphor to keep in mind for this. Although marriages of many permutations exist, here we're viewing marriage as an archetypal energy, the energy of union between two equal but opposite forces. Often the anima of a well-adjusted male who has a good balance between the masculine and the feminine presents itself as a beautiful woman or some other positive female archetype, in alignment with his current status in life. However, if the man has issues in developing the balance between his masculine and feminine natures, then his anima is likely to show up in his dreams as an inappropriate feminine energy, perhaps a mother, grandmother or witch-type figure, thus illustrating an unresolved issue that is causing an imbalance between the feminine and masculine within. The animus in a well-adjusted female is likely to be a gorgeous knight-in-shining-armour-type or otherwise a capable, friendly male, whereas if the masculine is undeveloped or imbalanced in the female, then that element is likely to show up as a frightening, brutal, weak or aggressive male character.

Here's one dreamer's attempt to balance her internal gender issues. The dreamer herself referred to this dream as an expression of her 'inner masculine cowboy':

I'm at a party with my cousin. She's wearing a beautiful sky-blue dress with lots of cleavage. She pulls up her skirt and says, 'Look.' Underneath the dress, she's wearing denim jeans and a pair of ugly black masculine shoes. Very practical, though.

'Why spoil the dress with those shoes?' I ask.

She doesn't answer, just lets the festive dress fall back with the ugly shoes sticking out from underneath it.

Six Gender Types

Within the two primary energies of the masculine and feminine there are six gender types that appear in dreams: the young self, the middle self and the wise self of both the masculine and feminine selves. These six within are all aspects of you. They mirror the six universal directions of north, south, east, west, above and below.

BASIC CHECKLIST OF MASCULINE/FEMININE CORRESPONDENCES

Gender Archetype	Meaning
Young girl	*Positive*: The inner child. The childish, playful element of the self. The virgin. Take time out to relax and play.
	Negative: Not taking responsibility for issues in life. Playing the victim. Stop messing around and grow up!
Adult woman	*Positive*: Following your intuition; being receptive, open, caring, nurturing and emotionally balanced. Collaborative community.
	Negative: Being overly submissive or overly aggressive. Anger issues, frustration, helplessness and confusion.
Old woman	*Positive*: Owning your power and wisdom, listening to the answers within. Sovereign energy.
	Negative: Not learning through experience, repeating old outworn patterns. Being weak and lacking in vital energy.
Young boy	*Positive*: The inner child. New adventures, The innocent. Carefree attitude, fearless innocence.
	Negative: Refusal to grow up – the Peter Pan syndrome.
Adult man	*Positive*: Focused, self-disciplined, accomplished, taking appropriate action. Right use of will. Building a legacy.
	Negative: Unfocused. Feeling powerless, lost, trapped. Messing things up. Being overly competitive, focused on winning at all costs.
Old man	*Positive*: Strength, courage, knowing who you are. The mentor.
	Negative: Loss of energy, lack of vitality. Shaky foundations.

Obviously, the above six characters can turn up in both sexes' dreams and we need to adjust the meanings in accordance with our gender.

These are just some basic issues that will appear. You can use other exercises in the book to get more specific about the qualities exhibited by your particular dream archetypes. But now it's time to get acquainted with them.

Getting Acquainted

Review one of your own dreams. You have to take the symbolic and translate it into the personal in order to unlock it. Everything in your dream is an aspect of you, but it plays out like a movie. Think of films, great epics, blockbusters – they always have archetypes, don't they? They have the heroine, the hero, the bad guy, the good guy. Most movies follow the hero's journey. That's what your dreams do too. They are just movies of your mind.

The characters in the movies are aspects of your personality acting out the different parts of you. Enjoy this discovery – it's fun. 'Oh, look, there's a bit of me I didn't realize I had.' Archetypes are a fascinating subject.

Remember, each of us has been steeped in the archetypal myths of our culture since we were young. We have all had fairy stories read to us. And we have a natural gift for recognizing and connecting to these fundamental energies. We just need that dreaming antenna to be tuned into the archetype channel.

Here's an extract from a workshop to help you identify your own archetypes:

✳ *'In this dream I saw a man standing in a nice environment surrounded by mountains. The place was sunny.'*

✳ *'Focus on the man. What was his character, what was he like? What can you remember about him?'*

✱ *'He was very quiet. He was meditating.'*

✱ *'That's the archetype of the wise old man, symbolizing the aspect of you that's your wise self. Where do you need to acknowledge and use your maturing wisdom in life? Do you need to take time out to meditate? You also had mountain imagery in your dream, which is another symbol representing the wise self. This dream is about you accessing your inner wisdom.'*

Making Connections

One of our primary human motivations is to connect. The next exercise taps into this by allowing us to connect with unresolved aspects of ourselves in a safe non-threatening and expressive way. Would you like to dance with your dream anima/animus?

DANCING WITH YOUR DREAMS

In this exercise you can work with any male or female dream character. My suggestion would be to work with one you find difficult or even repellent in some way.

Close your eyes and imagine a large empty dance studio. Music of your choice is playing.

See the dream character on the other side of the ballroom, some distance from you. You are the only two people here.

Your job is to encourage the dream character to dance with you. Maybe you have to flirt a bit or start dancing to encourage them to join you. Maybe you need to change the music or the type of dance to entice them. The dream character may ignore you or dance to a different tune. Do whatever you need to do to engage them in some kind of dance with you.

You may begin with a slow waltz whilst your dream character is head banging to their inner rocker. Don't judge or change what shows up, just let it resolve itself through the dance and the music. Ultimately you're aiming to get to a place where it feels good to be dancing with this stranger, where you feel complete.

When the dance is over, wriggle your toes and fingers, open your eyes and stretch.

Think of your dream character again and notice how your attitudes and feeling towards that archetype have changed for the better.

As always, complete the process by reflecting on what you've discovered and how it fits in with your current life circumstances. Is there some action you need to take because of what you know now?

This exercise can be used for any other dream characters that appear. You'll learn a lot about the nature of your archetypes by dancing with them. It will show you exactly how this energy connects with you and how you connect with it.

If you're dreaming about an archetype, then you need to bring some of the qualities of that archetype into your conscious awareness and into your waking reality. For example, if, as a female, I'm dreaming about an aggressive man, it's showing me that I'm not using enough of my masculine energy in my waking life. Perhaps I need to stand up for myself a bit more. Where could I use masculine energy in my life right now? Where do I need to be taking action? Where do I need to bring more of that male sense of foundation, structure and strength into my life? When I look at these issues and start to make changes, my dream becomes a powerful force for positive transformation in my life.

To illustrate, whilst writing this book I had a series of dreams where the common themes were strong female roles, strange unknown men, marriage and weddings. I understood from reviewing the series how I had to temper the relationship between my masculine and feminine selves in order to acquire the discipline necessary to produce a finished book. I was fully engaged with my feminine self, which allowed me to be inspired and dream, but didn't give me the masculine quality of action that was required to make those ideas and inspirations manifest. Hence my animus turned up as a series of ex-boyfriends trying to help in some way – but of course their help was inadequate, as they were ex-boyfriends for a reason. Other male figures were strangers to me, representing the masculine energy in its purest form that I was refusing to integrate, hence the recurring theme of marriage, illustrating how I needed to marry these two elements within myself in order to produce the result in my waking reality.

Now let's unpack a few more of your dream archetypes.

To begin with choose a dream from your dream journal, one that has some characters in it or maybe just one distinctive character. In this instance, don't look at the scenery, the background, just focus on the characters. I want you to see if you can pinpoint the archetypes represented by those characters. Is there a shadow side represented?

If you have a recent series of dreams you could look back and see if there are any common characters occurring that represent you, the persona, the face you show the world. The persona in Jungian terms is really the mask you present to the world. Where can you see that in your dream? It's not always obvious – it could be the helpful caretaker or the efficient executive, or it could be symbolized by an animal.

Is there somebody that is always helping everybody, the Florence Nightingale archetype? Or is there a manipulator, the trickster? Who's the bad guy?

Once you've identified a couple of archetypes, consider how they turn up in your dreams. What's their character like?

Are they always playing similar roles? What is the nature of that role? How do they interact with you, the dreamer? This begins to tune your attention into the archetypal energies they're acting out for you. Now you're ready to delve deeper into the motivations of your dream archetypes using this process of active meditation.

MEDITATION ON THE ARCHETYPE

You can do this exercise, based on Gestalt work, in two ways. Either you can merge with the dream character and speak from inside them or, if this feels difficult for you, you can see the dream character in front of you and interview them. This exercise is also interchangeable with symbols and you can work with it on an inanimate symbol as well as an actual character.

You may find it helpful to record these sessions and play back what you've said afterwards. That reflection of your exact words can reveal powerful new meaning at times. Otherwise, take notes as you go along if you can keep in a reasonably meditative state as you do so, or just record your insights at the end.

Choose the dream character/symbol you wish to know more about. Get comfortable, relax and close your eyes. Begin in the same way as all the dream visualizations by spending a few minutes consciously focusing on your breath and allowing yourself to deeply relax and soften your conscious awareness.

Now I want you to go back into the dream... Allow yourself to revisit it in your mind. Bring the character/symbol you're working with into your mind's eye. Bring the image really close to you... See the character standing before you as vividly and clearly as you can and now just step inside that character, become it. See and speak through their eyes and mouth...

Alternatively, let the character remain in front of you at a safe distance whilst you interview it.

Now I want you to speak as the dream character would speak. To begin with, maybe you could ask, 'What are you doing in my dream?'

Speak in the first person when you're speaking as the character or symbol. Always start 'I am...' For example, 'Who or what are you?' 'I am a house.'

If you're inside a symbol, what is the symbol saying?

If you're inside a person, describe your personality. In what ways are you like the dreamer and it what ways does your character differ from the dreamer's? Don't censor or judge your responses, just let them flow from the character.

Moving on now, still as this character or symbol, run through the following questions and answers:

✳ *'What is your purpose or function? What do you do?'* 'My purpose is to...'

✳ *'What do you like about being this dream symbol?'* 'I like...'

✳ *'What do you fear most as this dream character?'* 'I fear...'

✳ *'What do you most want as this dream character?'* 'What I want most is to...'

✳ *'What message do you have for me?'* 'I am here to let you know...'

When you've finished, step out of the dream character, wriggle your toes and fingers, open your eyes and stretch. Review what you've recorded or quickly record your insights now and reflect on how what you've written relates to the relationships and situations within your current life.

Finish by answering the following questions:

✳ And what do I know now?

> ✳ Is there anything else I now know?
>
> ✳ Is there an action I need to take as a result of this new information?
>
> These last questions are important, as they bring the message from the dream into our current life, and as we know, dreams are more powerful if we understand and act on the messages received.

Here's one dreamer's insights from this process. She was a young, very independent-minded single girl and her dream symbol was a kiss:

My purpose is to connect to others. I am feeling very giving. I'm here to show you how to let go of emotions and be more affectionate. I advise you to stop being so frozen and be more open. I'm here because it is time to show your affections. My purpose is to make you realize how easy and beneficial it is to let go of your feelings. My advice is to liberate your emotions. I am the part of you that you need to start revealing. I need to tell you that one kiss can to lead to emotional freedom.

These kinds of exercises and questioning techniques will give you an idea of the archetypes you're playing out. It's important to understand them, as they'll repeatedly show up in your dreams and your life. When you know them you can recognize what you're trying to balance out in life or what you're not paying attention to and address those issues.

Owning our Shadow

Integrating our shadow side is a necessary aspect of dream work. In fact, I would go as far as to say it is one of the primary functions of dreaming to bring to our awareness the disowned aspects of ourselves. These disowned parts of our psyche are what Jung termed our 'shadow' and they appear as dark archetypes in our dreams. Here are some examples, the first again from a workshop:

✳ *'I dreamed that someone gave me a baby and it was tiny. At first, it was sitting up in a box happily chewing on some bacon fat. I thought it needed liquids and this was its way of getting that. I don't know whether it was a boy or girl baby. I left it in my make-up case – by then it was even smaller – and I went upstairs to talk to Jane. She is somebody who did the shamanic course I did. When I came back to my room, there were three beds there and I was appalled to see that my bed was covered in clothes and in a real mess and I don't think they were my clothes. When I put my hand into my make-up case there was tremendous heat, especially from my new bottle of foundation. I realized the baby had a fever. I opened the bottle, but the baby was not in it, it was at the bottom of the case. I became very concerned, took the baby out and began to administer to it. I gave it the homoeopathic remedy belladonna and it looked just like a foetus.'*

✳ *'What archetypes can you see here?'*

✳ *'Well, the baby I think is probably my inner child.'*

✳ *'...and also the archetype of the innocent. We all have a pure self, so yes, the inner child and the innocent. The shadow also turned up in this dream. Belladonna represents your shadow aspect. The shadow and the innocent are directionally opposed opposites and in this dream they're interacting. You're feeding your innocent self your shadow self. This is about the integration of the shadow in order to become whole. It's interesting that you met Jane on a shamanic course. In shamanism harmony is achieved through the recognition, acceptance and integration of our shadow aspects. In this dream, you are attempting to do that. By giving belladonna to the innocent, to the baby, you're integrating your shadow. This is a fundamental process in allowing you to move forward, that's why the baby is returning to a foetus, and you linked it to your foundation and your identity, as clothes are symbolic of our identities out in the world. This is a classic Jungian example of coming into wholeness through the psyche of our dreams.'*

✳ *'How did you know belladonna was the shadow?'*

✳ *'What's belladonna?'*

✳ *'It's a homoeopathic remedy that comes from deadly nightshade.'*

✳ *'There's your answer: it's a dark remedy. A dark symbol in dreams will represent the shadow. This can be anything we fear, dislike or shy away from – a bat, a spider, a snake, a rat. But see how the shadow is not to be feared. It's not bad, it just is. You were healing yourself, using the homoeopathic remedy, by feeding the baby the belladonna.'*

Dark archetypes come in many guises:

✳ 'We are in a friend's apartment. There are a few people – at least one other woman. The apartment is fancy, modern, exquisite. The owner is my daughter's male friend. Stuff happens that I don't recall and I am alone in the apartment. There is a door leading down some stairs to a cellar. I walk down a couple of steps, but sense danger. I know that behind the door at the bottom of the stairs is a witch, and I don't have the courage to continue. Despite my protests, my daughter's friend returns and does go down to the witch. When he returns, he is obsessed by her. I fly and hide. I am very scared.'

✳ 'The mannequin is completely motionless and I start to relax. But then the hand twitches and I look at the

face and it has this horrible sly grin. I look at the doctor
who is sitting in a chair and he turns slowly towards me
and he too is a mannequin. He says, "Come on, there is
nothing to be afraid of." I am completely paralysed and
my heart is pounding, but I can't run away.'

✳ 'I'm running, terrified. There is a man with a gun chasing
me.'

✳ 'I'm faced by a mile-high black wave of water coming
towards me.'

When attempting this deeper work, remember dream answers
are *information* centred, not *you* centred, i.e. they're not
criticizing your ego. Yes, there will be aspects revealed that
your ego mind will baulk at, because it doesn't want to accept
that less than positive view of the whole Self and it tends to
take criticism personally! But if you can keep an impersonal
attitude and trust the information rather than your ego's huffy
assumptions, you'll make faster progress.

The key to understanding this work is the recognition that
at the Higher Self level, we're pure potential and we're all
One. Ultimately, we contain within us the potential to be both
the abuser and the abused. We cannot reach wholeness if
we're only prepared to accept the positive aspects of ourselves
without also accepting the negative aspects.

Sometimes our shadow is a nameless fear, which we'll
cover later under nightmares, but more often it appears as a
character or obstacle obstructing our path in some way. Here's
a wonderful dream of one man's integration of the shadow
within the dream. This dreamer had had unpleasant dreams
of his nemesis for over two years before this. This dream
illustrates the integration taking place within him:

*I was sitting at a small round table with my former nemesis on
my left and an unidentified old friend on my right. I was happily
introducing my nemesis to my friend, laughing and joking. It
was a surprisingly agreeable, charming conversation.*

'Dancing with our Dreams' (*see page 117*) is a great exercise to use to integrate the shadow within us, as is the following powerful technique, although you can do this exercise with any person that turns up in your dream.

DREAM CHARACTER EXERCISE

On a piece of paper, answer the following questions about the dream character you've chosen to work with:

* How would I describe this dream character?

* What qualities do they possess in order to be who they are and do whatever they are doing in my dream?

* How do I feel about them? (List all the feelings this character evokes in you.)

* What role do they play in my dream?

* For what purpose is this character in my dream?

Write down all the phrases or words that spring to mind. *Be honest* – no cheating! If you would describe them as manipulative, abusive and a control freak, then that's what you need to write down.

Now take each word or statement from the list you've just written and for each quality, attribute or role, answer the following questions:

* What part of myself is doing that to myself or someone else?

* Where or to whom do I do that, either to myself or others?

* Where in myself or with whom am I exhibiting this behaviour?

* How does this reflect the roles I play in my waking life?

To complete the exercise you can go through the list again and for each attribute ask, 'How has this behaviour served me?'

For example, if one of your words was 'controlling' and you recognized that there was a part of yourself that was always trying to control your weight, then perhaps that behaviour has served you by maintaining your health by not allowing you to become obese.

It requires huge honesty and courage to face ourselves squarely at this level. The rewards far outweigh the discomfort, though. When we can recognize, harmonize and heal these discordant elements in ourselves, then the nature of our relationship with others and the world around us automatically changes. As I mentioned earlier, you cannot change another, you can only change yourself.

If you're feeling really brave, you can do this exercise with anyone from your real life that you have an issue with. The more negative emotions you have concerning someone or something, the more likely it is to be a projection of some disowned aspect of yourself.

Celebrity Dreams

I often get asked what it means if you dream of a celebrity. For me, these are just our modern archetypes. In current culture, celebrity has become part of our collective myth. Through access to incessant global media we become steeped in the mythical lives of larger-than-life characters. Most of us don't truly know these people, they're not personal friends. But we think we know them and we feel a strong connection with their symbolic energy, as witnessed most clearly in the national outpouring in the UK after the death of Princess Diana. As with all archetypes, when you dream of a celebrity, look at the attributes and behaviour they exhibit. Do the 'Dream Character Exercise' (*page 126*) to reflect the messages back to yourself.

Here's an example from a woman who was struggling to find her way in her career at the time of this dream:

✳ *'I'm sitting with Angelina Jolie in the kitchen at a breakfast bar. We're just chatting. I've no idea what the conversation is about, but I notice that she has about three or four different washing machines and they're all oven height. They look like ovens but they're doing loads of laundry, the washing and drying of laundry. It is a really nice dream.'*

✳ *'What do you associate with Angelina Jolie?'*

✳ *'She always has projects on the go and she's a humanitarian. She's somebody I greatly admire. I think she's just a phenomenal person and a great actress. She's got everything anybody could ever want and she does it so well. The fact that the washing machines didn't look like washing machines but ovens was interesting. It was as if she was baking something, was always preparing something.'*

When this dreamer owned those aspects of the Angelina archetype for herself she could immediately see what she needed to take action on to move forward in her life, knowing that she already had 'everything anybody could ever want'. Powerful stuff!

Because the collective myth is part of us all, archetypal energies are relatively easy to tap into. We can travel with our minds to a place that allows us to access the archetype and seek information from it.

Let's end this chapter with a wonderful exercise for connecting to our dreaming archetype, our very own dream guide.

The Dream Whisperer

The Dream Whisperer is an archetype or character that allows us to get in touch with our dreaming mind. If you have an issue or a problem to solve, you can hand it over to the Dream Whisperer. You could even call on Morpheus, the god of dreams, to guide you through your dreamscapes. He is another dream guide who can help you interpret your dream symbolism and extract more meaning from your dreams.

The Dream Whisperer is a useful psychological mechanism that allows us to get out of our own way. Mostly, we *do* get in our own way. We're not good at giving ourselves permission to go to places outside our comfort zone and we resist experimenting with things that seem strange or out of the ordinary. We would far rather keep our head below the parapet, become invisible and conform to what we perceive to be the correct way to live through the example set by those around us.

If we hand over our responsibility to the Dream Whisperer, however, even though this is obviously another aspect of us, its effect is freeing. It lets us off the hook: 'Oh well, the Dream Whisperer knows what it's doing – I'll trust that. I may not trust all of myself, but I can trust that aspect of myself.' We can accept the make-believe aspect of the Whisperer. It overrides our internal critic, the part of ourselves that thinks we're no good or we can't do something or we're not bright enough or the myriad of other things that we use to put ourselves down. And it allows us a greater freedom to journey and to discover and explore different aspects of our psyche that we wouldn't normally allow our conscious mind to go to.

A lot of artists use this kind of technique. They just call it by a different name and it tends to have a human counterpart: it is the muse. In a sense the Dream Whisperer is your muse, it's your dream muse. It's what allows you to be inspired. It can give you that extra edge that ordinarily you wouldn't allow yourself to have.

Let's set out on a journey to meet your Dream Whisperer. Be aware that this archetype, just like each of us, has a dual aspect. In the journey this appears as two characters but in effect they are the light and dark aspects of the same being, not two different beings.

DISCOVERING YOUR DREAM WHISPERER

Take 10–15 minutes to enjoy this journey of discovery. Start by reading through and familiarizing yourself with the journey or record it and play it back to yourself. Leave plenty of pauses on the recording to allow yourself to explore the different journey stages.

Close your eyes, relax, breathe, meditate... Give yourself permission to journey and set your intention: 'To meet the Dream Whisperer within'.

Find yourself on a moonlit beach, with the full moon in the sky above, the waves gently lapping on the shore and soft, white sand beneath your feet. Walk into the warm sea and keep walking until you're submerged. You find you can breathe underwater easily and effortlessly. Swim deep, down into the ocean, deeper and deeper ... and even deeper than that ... deep down into the depths of the ocean until you come to the bottom of the sea and see an underwater cave before you.

Enter the cave and continue down its dark corridors until you come to a shimmering, mercurial mirrored door. Pause and see your truth reflected in the liquid surface...

On the other side of this door is your Dream Whisperer. Walk through the liquid mirror into a large underground cavern. Before you are two seats, one made of ivory and the other made of horn. Choose which seat appeals to you more and sit down.

As you look up, your Dream Whisperer appears in front of you. Spend some time now introducing yourself to this character, asking their name, getting to know them, asking them what dream guidance they have for you right now...

When you're ready, stand up and move to the second seat and again sit down. As you look up, the twin Dream Whisperer will appear. Get to know this character in the same way as the other. Ask their name and the nature of the guidance they have for you...

These two are one, the twin aspects of your Dream Whisperer archetype. The one representing the shadow dreams, the warnings, the behaviour we need to work on, is the guardian of the ivory chair. The one representing our future dreams and our knowing is the guardian of the horn chair.

Thank the dual aspects of your Dream Whisperer for their guidance and allow each to give you a dreaming gift now, one from each aspect...

Walk back through the liquid mirrored door and swim up through the cave and up, up, up through the ocean, back to the moonlit beach and come back into the now.

Wriggle your toes and fingers, stretch, have a quick shake and write down any insights, learnings and discoveries in your journal. Remember to note the symbolic dreaming gifts you received. If they seem mysterious, use the exercises from Chapter Five to unlock their symbolic messages.

Now you've met your Dream Whisperer, simply tune into them as you're drifting off to sleep and request their help in whatever dream endeavour you wish. Trust that the appropriate aspect will guide you, as they're both fully integrated within you. If you need a healing dream, a creative dream, a problem-solving dream or any other kind of dream, just ask. The more we know ourselves, the healthier we become, mentally, emotionally, physically and spiritually. We discover how to dance with life and stand in our truth, brave and free. That's the gift the Dream Whisperer brings you.

It's about applying the laws of magic to the small stuff – whatever you want to know. Why have your diets always failed? What's that nagging feeling you've got about your current relationship? Is this job/house/car the right one for you? Whatever the issue, the Dream Whisperer can help.

It does take practice and experience to understand our deeper selves. All of human life is about experience. It's not about knowledge, it's about experience. Knowledge comes *from* experience. You experience something, it proves to be true, you experience it again, it remains true – that's how you build trust in your world. It is a step-by-step process. So I encourage you to work on your archetypes. They're big keys to your dreams. If you're being chased by a monster, it's not a monster, it's your shadow, and you need to turn and face it. This is essential for bringing yourself into wholeness.

Now we're getting to grips with what our dreams mean to us we can begin to play with resolving some of the issues we are uncovering. The next chapter is all about how we can use our dreams to travel in time.

CHAPTER SEVEN

Playing the Time Game

Exploring your Dream Stream and Cosmic Diary

'The timeless in you is aware of life's timelessness; and knows that yesterday is but today's memory and tomorrow is today's dream.'
Kahlil Gibran

In dreams, time becomes an elastic concept. A dream can occur in *chairos* time, that is, sacred time or the eternal now. During sleep, the unconscious steps into this sacred time to bring wisdom, energy and insight from the eternal now into *chronos*, or chronological, time. This chapter deals with techniques, processes and exercises for playing with time. It offers tools to help you plan your life in conjunction with your Higher Self's inspiration. This is where the idea of dreaming your life into being really takes shape.

We're going to play with the concept of time, exploring how we can access our Cosmic Diary whilst awake and go there to change the effect of past events, set goals and clear negative dream emotions that can keep us stuck. As we'll discover, our dreams give us a framework for freedom without a structure that stifles.

Navigating Time

Sacred time is unlike linear time, where we have an obvious past, present and future – the yesterday, today, tomorrow concept. Sacred time operates across all dimensions. It's the eternal now. In sacred time there is only this moment and within that everything that ever was or will be already is. This is the gift of the present.

The Higher Self knows the cause of everything we have created in the universe. This is the continuous 'us' that crosses through time and space. Knowledge of both the future and the past is a function of the Higher Self because it created them. But we cannot always access our Higher Self. Our conscious mind decides what we want, but if our unconscious mind has a limiting belief about that, then the message never gets to the Higher Self; instead we receive a dream telling us what's in our way. However, as we'll discover, floating above our Dream Stream gets us in touch with the archetype of the Higher Self, which is where we need to be to influence the manifestation of our dreams. As Abraham Lincoln once said, 'The best way of predicting your future is to create it.'

Many scientists now agree that the universe is infinite. Each time we make a choice we create another dimension, another slice of infinity, a 'sliding doors' moment, if you like. Although it's a lot to take in, basically we are simultaneously living all the possible alternative realities that we can imagine for ourselves somewhere in the universe right now. If infinity is a given, then it can only be this way, because we are infinite too.

I think our dreams are the closest most of us get to really experiencing this concept. There we do visit other universes where we are someone else doing something very different. Although in the West it is accepted that dreams are just make-believe products of our creative brain functions, indigenous cultures view the dreaming mind somewhat differently. They believe we literally leave our bodies and travel to the different realms and realities that we experience in our dreams. The medicine people of Kenya, for example, will not wake a sleeper suddenly for fear of preventing the wandering spirit from re-entering the body. The Aboriginal tribe of Narrang-ga say that the human spirit can leave the body in sleep and communicate with the spirits of others, or with the spirits of the dead, who wander as ghosts in the bush.

To make this concept more real for you, pause for a moment and play with putting your mind anywhere in the world. Travel to the North Pole, check out the inside of a bucket on a cow ranch in Tennessee. Wherever we choose to put our awareness our extraordinary mind is there, in an instant. It doesn't matter if you have real experience of the place or not, your mind will take you there anyway (or at least your mental idea of it). Play some more: go and visit the inside of a black hole. What about the bottom of the deepest part of the ocean? Visit a star in outer space, or take a trip to Jupiter or Mars. You can take yourself there in your mind instantaneously. This is our awareness and it's entirely unlimited in its potential for travel. However, once it gets somewhere, it is fixed in that moment until it moves elsewhere. This fixing of our awareness in our personal 'now' is what creates our idea of reality.

Dreamtime Games

There are some rules for the dreamtime games we're going to play in this chapter, ones that we've already discovered in this book but are worth reminding ourselves of, as they are so vital to the enhancement of our personal well-being:

1. We have a conscious mind.
2. We have an unconscious mind.
3. We have a Higher Self or personal spiritual mind that is the source of all that is.
4. We can trust all of our minds.
5. Our unconscious mind (purveyor of dreams and gateway to our Higher Self) can and wants to communicate with us.
6. The unconscious mind works symbolically.
7. We can trust the first thing that comes up, however unusual it may seem.

Now we know the rules, here's a fun dream exercise to play with that will really help you to understand this concept of infinite time. Use this for any dream where you would like to know what happened next, any dream where you wake up before the crucial finale. Alternatively, take a dream that puzzles you in some way. Somewhere in the universe a dream twin, a second you connected to the same Higher Self, has completed that dream and knows what happened. This exercise is going to allow you to gain access to the information and experiences of that twin self to see how the dream panned out.

FINDING YOUR DREAM TWIN

Read through the instructions first so that you have them clearly in your mind. Then do the exercise.

Relax and bring to mind the dream you're going to work with and what you'd like to know about it.

Begin to imagine a dream twin somewhere in the cosmos who already knows what happened and can tell you when you find them.

Find yourself on the Bridge of Dreams, the bridge that takes you from the waking world to the dream world. Stand in the middle of the bridge, where you will notice a trap door in the floor. When that trap door opens you will jump through it to where your dream twin is.

Start to count backwards in your mind from 5 ... 4 ... 3 ... 2 ... the door is beginning to open ... 1 ... jump through.

Meet your dream twin on the other side.

Now allow this twin self to show you the answer to your dream. Remember you can ask questions of this dream self in the same way you would of any dream character. Spend a few moments exploring this dream world with your twin...

When you feel you have gleaned all the information you can, find yourself back on the Bridge of Dreams with the trap door shut.

Wiggle your fingers and toes and bring yourself back to the awareness of your body and immediate surroundings.

Write in your journal any insights, learning or discoveries.

You can also use this exercise to get advice on matters in your waking world. If, for example, you are stuck writing a report you can stand on the dreaming bridge and take a quick trip to find your dream twin who, somewhere in infinity, has already completed the report. Or you could go and find the successful you, the slim you, the rich you – the possibilities are endless.

The Dream Stream

We all have a way of storing time, all our past and future memories. This has been understood by ancient shamanic cultures since time immemorial, as NLP trainer Steve Andreas says in his article 'A Brief History of NLP Timelines':

*Every pattern has many antecedents, and most patterns
continue to be developed and refined after the first successes.
Philosophers have thought about time for millennia, even
before Heraclitus said, 'You can't step in the same river
twice,' some two thousand years ago.*

This concept of timelines has been brought into Western
awareness more recently through the work of people like
Peter McKeller, Tad James and Robert Dilts.

I first came to understand the structural basis of working
with time when I did my Master's in Timeline Therapy with
the Performance Partnership, based on the work developed
by Tad James and discussed in detail in the book *Time Line
Therapy and The Basis of Personality* by Tad James and
Wyatt Woodsmall. Although I have always understood time
travel in a shamanic sense, this material has allowed me to
create a unique synthesis of techniques, resulting in hypnotic
journeys that safely combine the creativity of dreaming with
the easy replicable structure of timelining. We're going to
use some of these journeying techniques for accessing sacred
time whilst awake. This will enable us to go into different
dimensions and levels of time and access the quantum fields.

We do know that many people have dreamed of things
in the future that they couldn't possibly have known about.
This presupposes that we must have knowledge of the future,
otherwise where does this information come from? Here's an
extraordinary example of a precognitive dream from gallery
owner Anna Hunter:

*Throughout my childhood I had a recurring dream in which
I was stabbed in my stomach. These dreams continued until I
was about 14 years old.*

*I would go to bed every night absolutely terrified of having
this very vivid dream, in addition to my visions of crocodiles
under the bed and a bear at the window. The dream was of a*

man stabbing me in my stomach. For years as a child I slept with my hands folded across my tummy. By the time I got to my late teens the dream had stopped and the crocodiles and the bear had gone too. However, years later, my son Sebastian, who was very sensitive, kept having frightening nightmares of police officers at the bottom of the stairs with something terrible happening.

On Friday 13 December 1991, at around 8.20 on a dark foggy evening I answered the door to a man who had dated my nanny a couple of times. He asked to come in and talk to me and lurched across the threshold with a knife and stabbed me in the stomach. He was mentally unstable. After the stabbing there were many police officers at the bottom of the stairs where I was sitting waiting for an ambulance to come. I was not expected to live and in fact I did die on the operating table. The surgeon felt it was miraculous that I survived. My attacker remains in a secure prison hospital.

We can all access our future, because we store all the events and dreams of our lives that have happened and have yet to happen in our own cosmic Dream Stream. But before we can begin journeying to access this, we need an idea of where our past is and where our future is in relation to our physical body.

CONNECTING TO THE COSMIC DREAM STREAM

Close your eyes and get into that dreamy, relaxed state you know is perfect for connecting to your unconscious mind. Remember it is your unconscious, instinctual response that we're looking for, not your conscious response. And it's your creative imagination you're accessing, so you can simply open your eyes at any time if you need to.

In that safe space of your creative imagination find yourself standing on the bank of a stream. The stream can be whatever shape, size, depth or direction feels right to you. It might be straight or meander or have sharp turns. Just notice its shape and direction and notice also whether it feels more comfortable and natural for you to stand looking at it equally in all directions or if you prefer turning to look either upstream or downstream. This is your personal stream of time, so now notice in which direction is the future and in which direction the past. And wherever the past and future come from is absolutely perfect for you.

Do you notice, now, that this difference in location of past and future memories implies some kind of organizational flow between those different memories?

Good. Now you're going to imagine floating safely and effortlessly above your Dream Stream in whatever way feels comfortable to you. Know that to feel more comfortable you can just float higher away from anything disturbing and towards the embrace of the energy of your Higher Self.

Look down and see the Dream Stream of your past and future memories flowing below you. Float back into the past and when you get there pause for a moment, turn and face towards now, and then float out over your future. Now float back over today and float down into the present day, wiggle your toes and fingers and bring your awareness back into the room you are sitting in.

From the perspective of psychological time, our conscious minds perceive or stretch time out to allow us to progress in a linear fashion from birth through to death. But if we let go of both ends of the time elastic it would ping back to the centre and just be this dot of time, the eternal now, the enormous nothing where everything resides. Now we have an understanding of our Dream Stream of time we can play in that cosmic playground and allow our unconscious mind to take us easily backwards and forwards through time.

This is akin to having a cosmic organizer in the sky. It works in the way in that you can go to your ordinary diary and rub out an appointment and change it for three weeks ahead because the person cancelled. Similarly, you can visit your Cosmic Diary and stick in a goal three weeks in the future, or go back to a memory and change the story you've been telling yourself about it.

Our understanding of memories isn't static. We remember them slightly differently each time we revisit them. Events happen in the moment. Whenever we look back on an event, it's similar but not the same. We can only process the past through our filter of the present. So what is truth? Truth is what you make it now. The only thing you can really change is now. The past and the future don't exist, that's why we can make change happen now.

Holographic Dreams

Everything is created in the now and we can transcend time. We're all one, though we experience each other as separate. Any time a group of people gather together they create a morphogenic field, or group consciousness. We can see this in stock markets, which create either a bull or bear market when critical mass of opinion is reached, often created by the media.

The morphogenic field is holographic in nature. If you keep ripping the picture of a hologram in half you keep getting a whole hologram rather than bits of it, i.e. the whole of a hologram is contained in every part and every part contains the whole. We need to understand that this is still a model of the world, albeit one with some serious scientific clout behind it, including David Bohm, a former protégé of Einstein's and a highly respected quantum physicist, and Stanford neurophysiologist Karl Pribram, one of the architects of our current understanding of the brain. As Pribram said, 'The human nervous system is a hologram of the universe.'

As Larry Dossey, MD, author of *Space, Time and Medicine*, writes;

This remarkable new way of looking at the universe explains not only many of the unsolved puzzles of physics, but also such mysterious occurrences as telepathy, out-of-body and near-death experiences, 'lucid' dreams, and even religious and mystical experiences such as feelings of cosmic unity and miraculous healings.

This is important to understand in relation to our cosmic dream work. Dreams are holographic; they seem real when you are in them and then not when you return to waking reality. Actually they're the same – it's your waking reality and your sleeping reality that perceive them differently, and that's just a matter of perception.

To understand how this works, bring to mind a vivid dream you've had. Close your eyes and really get back into that dream. Notice how it appears in your mind. See the dream movie playing out in full Technicolor, just as it happened in your dream.

Now clear the screen and think back to a recent holiday you had or party you attended. Play this movie in your mind just as it happened.

Reflect back on this experience. You'll notice that there is no significant difference in how your mind remembered the 'dream' and the 'real experience'. To your mind they're the same.

Think about the implications this has in terms of how we view our reality. It means our mind will process the emotions and memories of dreams in the same way that it will process the emotions and memories of reality. Consequently, we need to work on the negative emotions in our dreams, as they will affect us every bit as much as the emotions experienced in daily life.

Let's look at using time travel to clear old negative dream emotions.

Dreaming a New Dream

We can use our Dream Stream to go and visit past memories. We can go back to negative events and change our perception of those events in order to let go of the negative emotions we've held in relation to them. The key is finding the blessing or the positive learning in the experience. Once that occurs, we can let go of the emotions easily and effortlessly.

Think how quickly you can become angry. That's right, it takes only a few seconds. Well, we can let go of the anger, or any other negative emotion, that quickly too. Many of us think that it takes years to release our fear or anger. It doesn't. That's just another of the assumptions we have made up, the stories we have told ourselves. Feelings just need to be felt and then they can be released simply, easily and completely.

Let's do an exercise on letting go of negative dream emotions. This exercise is based on the shamanic concept of 'dreaming our dreams awake'. We can all choose to leave a negative dream behind and dream a new dream.

Any negative dream has four elements:

* the actual dream
* the memory of the dream (and we know how different those can be!)
* the emotions
* the learnings/blessings.

Once we have the learning/blessing we can release the negative emotion. Sometimes, though, the dream is so overwhelming we miss the learning and we need to go back and clear it so we can grow and develop. This is how this exercise works.

Follow the general advice for journeying given on page 19 when undertaking this process. In addition, you're well on your way to becoming a fully fledged expert of your own dream psyche now, so give yourself permission to journey deeply. Allow yourself to go to those places that are perhaps a little darker, a little more painful than you want to face. This is why having a facilitated process is sometimes helpful. It allows you to go deeper more easily. A good facilitator can look after the structure of the technique, allowing you to fully experience the journey. They also won't let you off the hook! Our ego mind can be excellent at forestalling our progress when we're working with ourselves. However, this journey is perfectly safe for you to do on your own if you're in good mental health. You might like to record it on tape and play it back or get a friend to read it to you. Work quickly. The whole process shouldn't take longer than five to ten minutes maximum and once you're used to it can be done in a few minutes.

You will get the best results if you find a comfortable place to sit or lie down and completely relax, somewhere where you will be undisturbed for 15 minutes.

As outlined below, this journey deals specifically with anger. This is an excellent generic journey to begin with, as most of us have experienced anger in our dreams. Once you are used to the technique, you can use it to clear out any other limiting beliefs you may have such as fear of success or negative emotions such as sadness, fear, guilt and anxiety. It is also perfect to use in conjunction with a power nap or daydreaming process (*see pages 232 and 76*) to double the benefits you receive from those precious daytime dream retreats (*see page 236*).

RELEASING NEGATIVE DREAM EMOTIONS USING THE DREAM STREAM

Become aware of your body as you start to get comfortable and relax. Ask yourself: 'Am I willing to release this anger now ... and for things to change? Am I committed to doing whatever it takes to successfully release it?'

If you don't get a strong immediate 'yes' to these initial questions, ask yourself what's stopping you releasing the anger. For what purpose are you holding on to it? How is this anger serving you? Are you willing to let it go now? Good.

Focus on the physical sensations inside your skin. Visualize the dream and the action that produced the anger. Become aware of how you believe the anger is there. How do you know this anger has been true for you until now?

Notice the bodily feelings of this knowledge. It's always been there, it's just you've never tuned in and noticed it before, and now you can. You don't need to understand this knowing or analyse it, just be with it. You're going to take that awareness into the journey and follow it back to its root cause, the original source, in order for it to be released easily and effortlessly.

Now enter your sacred imaginative space, your dreamtime, and find yourself standing comfortably on the beautiful bank of your personal Dream Stream. Now, as before, float up above your Dream Stream, remembering this lovely spot as the point in time that you call 'now'. Remember you can instantly come back to this spot and return to waking reality whenever you want.

When you're as high above your Dream Stream as you feel comfortable with, remaining safely at that height or even higher, let your Higher Self guide your unconscious mind directly back to the root cause, the original event in the past that will allow you to let go of this anger easily and effortlessly.

As you float safely back above your Dream Steam you may become aware of other related events that also occurred in your past. Just notice them and move on until your unconscious mind brings you to a stop safely above the root-cause event.

If you wish to instruct your unconscious mind to jump directly to the root cause, since it knows where it is and time doesn't exist here, it can do that for you. Go right back to the root cause, the original event in the past that will allow you to let go of this anger easily and effortlessly. This may be a time in this lifetime or before. Trust your unconscious mind to take you to exactly the right memory now.

When you're there, from this safe space, look down into your Dream Stream and notice the location of the root cause event.

Now float down into that event and briefly acknowledge the event and the emotions your unconscious mind has stored in that event for your safety.

Now come out of the event and float back up ... way, way above your Dream Stream and travel way, way back along your Dream Stream to a time before this dream event ever occurred, or any of the dream events that led to this dream, and now, from this place of safety and connection to your Higher Self, turn and face your dream emotion. Ask what its positive intention for you is. What's the blessing in disguise that will allow you to let go of this emotion, easily ... effortlessly ... now? That's right, that's the one...

Is there a colour associated with that blessing? A sound? A feeling? If so, and whatever colour, sound or feeling you get is perfect for you, inhale that colour into your body, through the crown of your head and exhale that colour through the soles of your feet. Continue to do this for a few, calm relaxed breaths. Hear the positive sounds and feel the positive feelings.

Look towards your future and flood your future memories with this colour, sound and feeling, seeing how they change in light of this new information.

Now look way, way in front of you and below you at that old dream and notice that the emotion has released from your body. You may still have the memory of the dream, but you will find you no longer carry the emotion in your body.

If the emotion hasn't completely disappeared now, that simply means that there are other blessings that your unconscious mind wants you to get so you'll be safe, so simply give your unconscious mind permission to give you all the blessings you need and you'll know that you've received them now because the emotion will have completely disappeared. Good.

Now you can safely float down into that old event and experience for yourself that all the negative emotion that was there a few moments ago has disappeared. It's completely gone now.

Now float back up and, staying nice and high, float along the Dream Stream back to now. If you encounter any memory with that old negative emotion along the way, simply breathe the blessing colour into it and continue to do that until all the negative emotion in the memories disappears, all the way back to that wonderful place on the bank of your personal Dream Stream and back into your physical body. Wiggle your toes and fingers and become aware of the environment around you and what time and day of the week it is.

Here's one dreamer's feedback from this process:

I am in a red sports car, with an open top, and my girlfriend is in the car and she is squeezing me, sitting over me as I try to steer ... and we veer across a wide main road and I am on the wrong side, and I have to get back and round the traffic lights. We manage it and get across and up the hill to ... I think the hospital ... and we turn left into a drive and I get out and it's the wrong place.

Working on this in our dream group, I gained an understanding that I allow myself to be squeezed out, I overcrowd my life with people, some of whom drain my energy, and I let them. I took this as an old pattern that I took down my Dream Stream yet something else became evident...

I went back in time to my grandmother on my maternal side, who had twins, my mother and her sister Irene, in 1918. At the time she didn't know she was having twins. It was only after the first, Irene, was born, that the doctor noticed another baby. My mother (an aspect of me) was feeling squeezed in the womb and came out 15 minutes later.

The message for me was that a pattern of being squeezed out in my life was coming down my cellular history and now I feel that by letting this go, I am released.

When doing this process with clients, I have found that some people get very specific data. I was doing this journey with someone recently and they went back to 3 o'clock in the morning on a starry night in 586 BC. It was that clear and instant. However, somebody else might get yesterday afternoon in this current lifetime. This process doesn't presume a belief in past lives nor does it reject the possibility. We have access to all these different memories and all these different moments in time on a biological, cellular level. Each baby that's born spends nine months absorbing the cellular memory of both parents *ad infinitum* down the ancestral line.

The above memory could have been some past DNA, because somewhere we carry the DNA, the molecular structure and cellular memory of all our ancestors. By revisiting that memory the client was able to release the emotions trapping them in the memory and create a fundamental shift in their behaviour in their current life. That's the power of working with your dreams.

Some of you may be thinking that going back and changing a memory or a story mentally is simply ignoring the reality of the event. But what's reality? It's impossible to know. As we've discovered, we can't control the events that happen to us in life – they're the facts – but we absolutely can change our responses to them and the meaning and the emotions that we've told ourselves about them, and that changes our reality.

Here's a personal example to illustrate. I come from a violent alcoholic background. For years I told that story with ferocity, clinging to my version of events, considering myself to be damaged goods and believing I had a right to be angry and aggressive as a result. I was an angry young woman for many years until I realized I could do something about it. I wore that 'bad' childhood as a badge of honour, in reality using it as an excuse to stop myself being who I truly was. The day I woke up to the fact that I'd simply made up how I felt about what happened to me suddenly released me. It gave me back my power to change my story, my perception of events and thereby my future outcomes.

The first thing I noticed that changed was the fact that I never told the story of my childhood again. It had lost its hold on me. It was simply no longer relevant. It no longer defined who I was. I was free. Instead of perceiving myself as a victim, which I'd done for so long, I re-evaluated the experience as a learning experience, one that had enabled me to empathize with clients and made me stronger and more determined in life. In fact, my tough beginnings have proven to be an enormous blessing in my reconstruction of the story. The facts are the facts. What happened still happened. I can't change that, but I can and have changed the story I made up about it, and doing that has changed my life.

Putting a Goal into your Cosmic Dream Diary

We've played with the past to resolve negative emotions and limiting beliefs; now we're going to fast track to the future to play with manifesting our dreams.

In the same way that you can alter entries in your normal diary, you can play with the entries in your Cosmic Diary and manifest a dream you'd like to see come true. When we're clear on what we want, our energy moves towards our goals. When we're not, it loses power and gets dissipated.

To start this dream-manifesting process, set your intention. This is vital for rewriting future memories. What do you want to have happen? What dream would you like to materialize?

If you can't think of a goal, ask yourself the following questions and find the common elements:

* What would you do if you were given six months to live?
* What would you do if you suddenly had tons of money and never had to worry about losing it again?
* On a scale of 1–10, where 1 is nowhere and 10 is complete success, how close are you to achieving your goal? Go with the first number that comes into your head.
* On a scale of 1–10, how confident are you that you can achieve this dream?
* If it's less than 10, what would make it a 10?
* What's the one thing you know you need to do now to set this dream in motion?
* What help or resources do you need to make this dream come true?
* If there were three essential things that absolutely had to happen for this dream to materialize, what would they be?

Now incubate a night-time dream around this goal. Sleep with the goal under your pillow and record any dreams you get, or even just fragments or feelings. When we work on our internal dreams, our external dreams tend to manifest with far greater ease. I suggest you give the ideas at least a couple of nights' incubation for best effect.

My research suggests that the dreaming mind continues to respond to requests over a period of two or three nights of dreaming. This first stage will bring to the surface any negative assumptions or issues that are blocking your dreams. You can then clear these using the Dream Stream process (*see above*), which will ensure your dream really does come true.

You could stop the process there or, once you have a clearly defined intention or goal, you can supercharge its potential to manifest by entering it in your Cosmic Dream Diary. If you already know your goal you can skip the incubation above and just enter the goal in your Cosmic Dream Diary. To do this, we'll journey to the upper world to visit our Higher Self. Again, you may like to tape this journey first and play it back to yourself. First set a date by which you wish this goal to be accomplished. An exact date is best.

VISITING THE COSMIC DREAM DIARY

Relax, take some calm deep breaths and find yourself in a garden, the garden of your mind.

Somewhere in this garden you will find an ancient tree. Enter this mythic Tree of Life and pause for a moment before allowing your mind to travel, up, up, up, out through the branches of the tree above your life. Travel upwards until you reach the Kingdom of Light, where all future memories and possibilities reside. Your goal already exists, completed, by you, in a parallel dimension. In some other slice of infinity it has already happened.

State your intention to the guardian of this kingdom, who will escort you to the memory you seek. Clearly see yourself having completed the task in this vision. See yourself in front of you, telling you what action you now need to take in order to complete your goal. Know that you will remember this action clearly.

Ask for any other advice you need to accomplish the goal ahead. Take this picture of your completed goal and step into it. Look through your own eyes and feel what it feels like to have your heart's desire. Feel what you feel, see what you see and hear what you hear. Make this picture compelling, as vividly real as possible.

Now step out of that body and see yourself achieving the goal in front of you. Fix this scene of your completed goal in your mind.

Now take that picture and follow the guardian along a corridor until you reach a door with your name on it and the words 'Cosmic Diary Room'. Only you have permission to enter this room, this is your cosmic PDA, no one shares your exact vibrational frequency. Only you can access your memories.

Enter the room and see a giant pictorial calendar on the wall. It vibrates slightly and everything is in motion, as all memories are variable until the moment of realization. Take the picture you have and walk along the screen in the direction of your future until you see the specific date you set earlier for your goal to be accomplished. Insert the picture right in this spot. Click your fingers over the page to seal it in. (You may like to do this in reality, too, as the noise helps glue the intention in place.)

Now turn and look towards now, seeing all the memories between then and now change in light of this new memory. Leave the diary room and follow the guardian back to the

> *gates of the kingdom and begin your descent back into now.*
>
> *Float all the way down, down, down, through the sky levels and the heavenly levels, down through the branches of the tree back into the trunk and your body, and back into the room, right back to today, back to now.*
>
> *Wiggle your fingers and toes and state the day, date and year to yourself when you come back into the room.*
>
> We need to stay in the present, because this is where we live and need to be able to function. It is highly unlikely you'll ever get lost in time, though — the most that might happen is you could feel a little ungrounded or disorientated.
>
> Now stand up slowly and give yourself a thorough shake.

TOP TIP

Shaking the flesh loose off the bones for a few minutes is a brilliant technique for shifting your energy any time of day, especially if you're feeling tired and haven't got time to take a nap.

Congratulations, you've just made your first Cosmic Diary appointment for the realization of your dreams. Write down any messages you received from the self that had already completed the task and take the action that was recommended. Or, if that is not possible, take a step towards being able to take that action. This last step is absolutely essential. These processes absolutely work. But if we do not follow them with action in the real world, they will have limited use.

The difference is you're now taking *inspired* action rather than just doing any old thing that comes to mind or what somebody else has told you will get the job done. You'll soon

discover there is a world of difference, not only in terms of
the pleasure you'll get from taking the new actions, but in the
results you'll achieve as well. Suddenly you're following your
own inner wisdom easily and effortlessly. You're allowing
your magnificence and truth to shine. Your unique way of
being in the world is beginning to show up and nothing can be
more perfect than that!

I encourage you to play with the techniques given in this
chapter. Their power grows with regular use. With practice,
you can also get much faster and more efficient at using them.
Often I will do an inner journey process whilst whiling away
time on a tube journey or standing in a queue. When you
understand them and have practised them, you can easily do
this too.

CHAPTER EIGHT

You're Not Alone

Exploring Common Dream Themes

'We are not only less reasonable and less decent in our dreams ... we are also more intelligent, wiser and capable of better judgment when we are asleep than when we are awake.'
Erich Fromm

A fascinating thing about dreams is their commonality across all places and peoples. Not only do we share common daytime experiences but common night-time ones as well. This is the beauty of the human condition. We get to experience the unique individual aspect of self and, simultaneously, the connected, shared experience of others. It has been well documented that people of different age, sex, country and culture share the most common dream themes of dying, falling, flying, nakedness, being trapped, teeth falling out, etc. These dream themes relate to our primordial experience of life, to those base fears and common experiences we all share. As we become immersed in dream interpretation, we'll recognize those that appear in our own dreams and alert us to the primal fears and anxieties that are being triggered within us. Some of the most common ones will be explored here.

Losing Teeth

This is an extraordinarily common dream across the world. It is a primal fear of survival dream, an archetypal experience that spans dream consciousness across all cultures. Without teeth, we cannot eat. Moving from one state of being to another can also threaten our survival, so generally it is a reflection on transiting from one life stage to another. This is the universally shared meaning of the dream.

The meaning for you personally can only be understood in relation to the specific transition currently taking place in your life. You may be leaving home for the first time, for example. Separation from parents is a necessary rite of passage that every young person has to undertake and often provokes losing-teeth dreams. Indigenous tribes help themselves through this process by conducting rituals around the separation process. This connects the individual fear to the universal experience and allows the individual to feel connected and less alone.

Here's a classic teeth dream from a 16-year-old girl:

I was in my parents' room with two of my friends and suddenly my teeth were all wobbly. I decided to pull one out. It came out easily but afterwards a nerve from the tooth was hanging out of my mouth. I pulled it out and it seemed to be a long piece of metal.

Then my neighbours came round for tea. My good-looking neighbour tried to talk to me, but every time I tried to speak, my teeth would fall out, and I couldn't communicate.

If this dream occurs, ask yourself:

* How is my survival being threatened?
* What am I scared of losing?
* What can't I digest?

✳ What is fundamentally changing in my life?
✳ What are the unnamed fears I can't talk about?

Flying Dreams

Flying is another globally common dream theme. However, there are different views on its meaning. Freud felt that it symbolized sexual intercourse, whereas Jung felt that it represented upcoming and profound life changes. T. C. Brink, a Californian psychologist, related flying dreams to an increase in self-confidence, sense of freedom and creativeness, and several contemporary psychotherapists have reported that clients who are beginning to rise above their current circumstances frequently report flying dreams.

I agree with all those different interpretations and for me flying dreams essentially relate to our primal desire to escape the restrictions of our physical limitations. To feel free and unfettered is our soul's primal urge. The spirit within us wants to stretch its wings.

When I ask clients the questions about what they would do if they had six months to live or won the lottery, the number-one response is: 'I'd travel.' With the six-months-to-live question it is a direct, instant answer; with the lottery win there is often the occasional procurement first – new house or a holiday – then travelling. Most people don't even have a clear idea of what countries they'd visit. It's more the primal urge to explore, to discover, to feel free to move that is driving their response.

It is a primary human desire to go beyond what is known in the hope of discovering true knowledge. It is a reflection of our need to conquer ourselves. Those that manage it – the yogis, Zen masters and shamans – find peace. Then the mind is stilled. The impersonal becomes known. When we take the 'I' out of our ego, the equation changes and all conflict evaporates. Our life is just free-flowing experience. Existential existence. It just is.

Here are some examples of flying dreams:

✴ *'I jumped and realized I could fly...'* This dreamer feels the need to escape and has the power to do it.
✴ *'I was hovering just above the ground and could go anywhere I wanted.'* This dreamer doesn't need to fly too high to get anything they want.

Another aspect of flying dreams is gaining new perspectives. We fly above to be able to get a better view. When these dreams arise, ask yourself:

✴ What do I want to escape from?
✴ Why am I not feeling free?
✴ Where am I losing perspective?
✴ Where do I need to look at things differently?

Transport

Transport in dreams is about your journey through life. The type of transport that appears will say a lot about how you negotiate your life. If you're running in a dream, providing you're not running away from something, it's normally positive. You're on your own two feet, you're healthy, you're physically fit because you can run and you've got energy to do that. If you're walking, you feel good about yourself and you're using your own resources to get somewhere. It's not quite as powerful as running – you like to take time to meander through life. If you're on a bus that's stuck or in a car that's broken down, however, your life journey is being thwarted in some way. What's stopping you?

Cars are very individual forms of transport. If you dream a lot about them, you're following your own path – you're not getting on the bus with everybody else. How is the car travelling? Is it speeding? (Do you need to slow down?) Are you driving it? (Are you in control?) Or is somebody else driving it? (Have you handed over the reins of your life to someone else?)

Trains are a fast, generally reliable, form of transport. They're quite smooth and indicate you're on track in life. But you are travelling in the company of other people, so are not making your way individually. This might be fine – you might be working in a company, for example. If trains turn up, ask:

✻ Where am I on track?
✻ Where am I going off the rails?

Look at every aspect of the dream journey and reflect back to your current life to get the advice being offered.

Here are some examples of how transport can arise in dreams:

✻ *'He was driving me along a road 500 feet above sea level. Without warning, he swung the steering wheel to the left and plunged us far down into the sea.'* Here we can see the dreamer is letting their past emotional memories take over their journey and throw it off course. The sea represents the emotions and memories and the left tends to relate to feminine issues and our intuitive side.
✻ *'I was in a big silver Merc. I was driving...'* This dreamer is travelling through life in style, in their own individual and powerful way.
✻ *'I decide to run. I feel strong, I'm jogging. There's no one there, it's like a desert landscape. There's a long straight road ahead and I'm just jogging strongly along this road, directly upwards.'* This dreamer is progressing in life strongly and directly, but are they too isolated?
✻ *'I've had lots of taxi drivers, I've had taxi drivers consistently, and buses...'* This dreamer is being chauffeur driven through life, but veers between the luxury of the taxi (easy, direct, fast and expensive) and the stop, start

chauffeuring of the bus (more hassle, less direct, slow and cheap).

∗ *'I'm dreaming of being on horseback...'* Horseback is a powerful way to journey. It requires dependency on another but also implies a good working partnership. Do you like to do things with someone else? Do you find it difficult to do things on your own?

∗ *'I'm waiting for the jet to take off.'* Where is your life waiting to be jet-propelled?

People and Relationships

The desire to connect and be in relationship is another fundamental human need. All of us enter into relationships, hence we'll all experience social interaction of varying kinds in our dream worlds and isolation in our dreams when we're feeling disconnected and alone.

We've discussed some of the basics concepts of relationship already in the archetype chapter. Here we're looking at other relationships in dreams. For example, research suggests twice as many women as men dream of sleeping with celebrities. This isn't that surprising when we know that dreams reveal our deeper truths. In the West, women are taught to keep quiet about their lust objects whilst men are more upfront about potential conquests. And what we can't express openly, we'll tend to dream about. Women also read more prolifically about celebrities, and celebrity magazines are very much geared to the female market. Our dreaming mind uses images from our personal database to populate our dreams and so celebrities are likely to reappear in women's dreams.

A celebrity can be a useful symbol, as this dream illustrates:

I dreamed I was married to Paul McCartney and he made me a cup of tea in a chipped mug with no handle... (I'm not a fan of his at all and I'm happily married.)

This dream is unrelated to the woman's real marriage. It is indicating she has not fully reconciled with the masculine within her. It is not currently up to scratch. It's chipped, with no handle, a shoddy offering from someone she's not particularly a fan of. The unconscious mind is suggesting this woman take herself in hand if she wants to make progress in life and accept herself for all that she is.

Another primal human urge is the urge to express our sexuality. We're all sexual beings. We often have sexual dreams when we're not getting enough sex in real life. This is the body's way of relieving its frustrations. We'll also often dream of old lovers when we're embarking on a new relationship. Our vulnerability in love will bring our insecurities and relationship issues to the surface and our dreams will highlight those concerns for us.

Either rejection or acceptance in life can turn up in our sex dreams. We'll also often dream of sexually taboo subjects. This is just our psyche exploring elements within ourselves that we need to integrate, not a reason to worry that we might be secretly perverted. If you're dreaming of having sex with your mother, check out where you need to be mothered or adopt a more nurturing attitude to others; don't book a session at the therapist's! As we know, our dreams are always about harmonizing our discordant elements.

If you're a virgin in your dreams, ask yourself what first experiences or new beginnings are happening in your life. Great dream sex can often arise when you have something to celebrate in life, perhaps an unexpected win, a new job, a promotion, a new baby, etc. Conversely, if you dream of impotence, maybe you feel you're falling short of the mark in some area.

Here are a few examples of relationship dreams:

* *'I'm dancing in a ballroom with a stranger.'* This dreamer is integrating the masculine elements within her. How can she use more of her unused masculine energies in real life?

* *'I am a soon-to-be bride but I am dreaming of my boyfriend jilting me at the altar.'* Where are this bride's insecurities stemming from? Are they normal anxiety or deeper fears?

* *'I'm dreaming of cheating on my husband with my husband!'* Does this woman desire more sex with her husband? Or is she denying some aspect of the masculine within herself?

Sharing dreams in relationships will help us relate to each other better by allowing us to understand the motivations, emotional responses and underlying assumptions of our partner.

Identity Issues

Our desire to fit in is a primal motivation. We cannot survive alone, so we become adept at adapting to our environment in order to be accepted. How well this is working or not working for us will definitely be revealed in our dreams, generally with symbols and images of clothes, the 'identity kit' we use to fit in and feel accepted.

I got arrested at the airport because my suitcase was full of all my stage clothes and stuff. Customs wouldn't believe that I hadn't bought them abroad. I was getting angry and frustrated, saying, 'These are my clothes. I've had them for a long time. Some of them are older than you,' but the official wouldn't let me through and I was getting so frustrated I was going, 'But they're mine! I'm not moving, I'm going to stay here. I'm not moving.' He said, 'We can take them off you and you can go through,' and I said, 'No.'

I realized that this was about me holding on to things and not letting go.

* *'I was worried about clothes for work.'* Check out your identity. How are you showing up at work? Do you fit in? Do you feel uncomfortable at work?
* *'There were piles of old clothes…'* Ask yourself, 'What part of me is carrying an old identity? Where do I need to change my persona?'
* *'I found a bathroom. I don't know why, but I needed to put foundation on and do my make-up and stuff. Yes, I definitely had to get dressed up.'* Where is this dreamer needing to put on a face to the world?

Recurring Dreams

Recurring elements are the most common dream genre of all, but it is not until we begin to write dreams down and periodically review them that we discover their real juice. Then we realize that instead of being random nonsense, our dreams have themes, patterns, continuations, progressions and resolutions. However, these gifts do not yield themselves without the written evidence.

Recurring dreams are basically trying to tell you something new about something old, something stuck. When you understand the meaning, the dream changes or disappears. With recurring dreams it's important to pay attention to what stays the same and what changes. These elements will be clues to where things are changing and shifting in your life.

In our conscious minds we can easily remember events and spend time in the recapitulation process. This is where we need to resolve any energetic blocks to our flow from erroneous past assumptions and repressed emotions so that we can move forward. Shamans across the world believe this process of recapitulation is essential for our growth and development. Hence it is important to observe our dream process over time as it will highlight the unconscious assumptions that require resolution.

For example it was not until I reviewed a two-year period of dreams (I do not record dreams every night) that I realized I often dreamed of being in an old people's home. Because this setting was not especially relevant in the context of the unfolding drama of the dreams, I hadn't clocked the recurrence of the theme. However, having seen this pattern it became extremely relevant to me, as old people's homes have a particular significance in my life in that I was brought up in one as a child. These dreams now clearly encapsulate aspects of childhood that I can review and learn from because I recognize the dream language.

We may have common humanity, but each of us has our own way of interpreting reality and interpreting our dreams. Professor Antonio Zadra of the Montreal Dream Laboratory collected thousands of dreams and converted them into numbers in order to see how often people dreamed about certain topics. He ultimately discovered that his research was more beneficial for the individual in revealing the patterns of their personal psychological development than in revealing any dreaming consensus among the general populace. Our dreams are where our true uniqueness lies. Therefore, whilst it is useful to explore common themes in order to understand our more primal urges, as with all dream work, ultimately we need to refer our discoveries back to ourselves.

Here are some examples of commonly recurring dream themes:

* *'I have a recurring dream that when I try to talk, my mouth starts to fill up with stones, gum and other different things, which stops me from talking. I try to pull the stones, etc. out of my mouth, but it keeps filling up. I can pull out handfuls of the stones, but it still doesn't allow me to talk.'* Is this dreamer speaking before thinking? Are they saying too much? What are they afraid of saying? What do they need to say that they feel they can't?

* *'I have recurring dreams of headless people.'* Where is this dreamer not paying attention to their thoughts when this dream appears? Or are they acting like the proverbial 'headless chicken'?
* *'I have a recurring dream that my house is flooding and I'm trying to save photos.'* This dreamer feels emotionally overwhelmed by something that's happened in the past that they'd like to have held on to.
* *'I have a recurring dream that I'm in my car going uphill. It gets steeper and steeper until I feel the car will flip over and my kids will get hurt.'* A natural mother's anxiety dream. Am I a good enough mother to keep my children safe?

The following exercise helps us to resolve recurrent themes without the need to consciously understand them.

CHANGING THE DREAM GAME TO RESOLVE RECURRING OR DISTURBING DREAMS

You can do this exercise several ways: in your mind or written out on a piece of paper or with a partner. If you work with a partner, you relate your dream out loud and your partner says, 'Change,' out loud whenever they feel appropriate and at that moment you change the story as illustrated in the example below. All the methods work successfully, so do whichever feels right for you.

* Find a quiet place to relax where you will not be disturbed for 10–15 minutes.

* Take a few long, slow, quiet deep breaths into your belly and allow all your muscles to totally relax. Whatever happens during the exercise is exactly right for you.

* Begin to tell yourself the story of your dream in the present tense, e.g. 'I am walking down a hill in a pink overcoat.' Each time you get to a moment in the dream where something

> uncomfortable happens or the recurring element occurs, say the word 'Change' loudly in your mind. At that point, you simply change the scene in your mind.
>
> Here's an example to help you understand the process:
>
> *I am walking down a hill in a pink overcoat.* Change. *The road is flat and I am wearing a blue tutu. I continue along this road and then find myself trapped inside my old family home.* Change. *I am flying along the road towards my new home, feeling fantastic. I am seeing a massive storm brewing outside the window of my home, which feels very menacing.* Change. *I can see a beautiful sunrise, the beginning of a brand new day rising over a calm blue sea. I feel optimistic and happy.*
>
> * When you get to the end of the dream, repeat the above process two or three times with different scenarios each time you say 'Change.'

Often dreams are compensating for something we do not have in our waking reality or we are not actioning in our waking reality. They help the psychological processing of whatever we're not dealing with. Again, the question to ask is: 'For what purpose is this dream occurring at this time in my life?'

Wish-fulfilment

Dreams respond to desire. Hence there are such dreams as wish-fulfilment dreams. These tend to have a particularly distinct quality. They usually stand out from other dreams. They're dreams such as winning the lottery, flying over the world, being on a luxury holiday or being married to someone rich and famous. They're escapism dreams. They're lighter, more optimistic in nature than our usual dreams. They are our dreaming mind giving us some time off and connecting us to our deeper desires.

Dreams do have different levels of meaning and application and these dreams can be pure pressure-release dreams. If there's a lot going on in your day-to-day life then the dreaming mind can let you play in God's playground and fly around several cosmoses and universes for a few hours and you'll feel better when you wake up, with a renewed sense of optimism, a new perspective and fresh hope. My giant dream-catching spaceship dream is a case in point. There was a wonderful feeling of relief and excitement when I woke from that dream. I'd had great fun roaring round the universe in charge of my own spaceship!

Normally how you feel when you wake is a good clue to the nature of the dream. Wish-fulfilment dreams tend to make you feel good. If you *don't* feel good, check out those negative emotions and investigate what's beneath them. As with any dream, it's always worth investigating the symbolic meanings behind the images you receive. Why are you dreaming of winning the lottery? Are you feeling trapped in your current situation? Do you need to take time out and rest and relax? Is this the reason for the holiday images?

Toilet Dreams

Toilet dreams are symptomatic of what we need to let go of in life – usually emotional baggage. It's an obvious metaphor. Going to the toilet is a shared human experience – we all have to eliminate waste matter.

Some examples:

* *'I'm on the toilet outside with people gawking at me.'*
  Do you have issues about being exposed? What are you embarrassed about?
* *'The toilet was not plumbed in and there was no washbasin. Then there were workmen with stepladders fixing a light bulb. I left. I had to make my way across the*

far end of the room to the toilet.' Is this dreamer wanting
to let go before being ready?

* *'As I sat on the loo, to my left there was a large bin. I went
to put something in it and there was a man's body inside. It
wouldn't fit in properly.'* Where does this dreamer need to
get rid of her overly masculine nature?
* *'I go to the toilet and do a very runny poo and the water
overflows and there are also loads of used tampons
overflowing with the crap.'* This dreamer has no problem
letting go, but is doing so in a way that is uncomfortable
and exposed. Do they have verbal diarrhoea? Do they
emotionally offload on everyone else?

Nakedness/Exposure

We need shelter to survive. Exposure dreams stem from this
primal anxiety within us and translate into our modern ways
of living:

* *'I'm naked on stage waiting to take an exam.'* Is this
dreamer feeling unprepared in life? Are they feeling tested
in some way?
* *'I run out the house because I'm naked. He comes
out and I say, "Sorry, don't look. Just wait a minute, I
need to put clothes on."'* Where is this dreamer feeling
embarrassed in front of others? What part of themselves
are they hiding?

If nakedness dreams occur, ask yourself, 'Where am I feeling
vulnerable? Overexposed? Unprepared? Not ready?'

Animals/Birds/Insects

We're not alone on this planet, we share it with other
creatures. Animals represent our basic instincts in dreams,

the beast within. Some fascinate us, some can kill us, some delight us and others are pests and irritants.

When animals, birds and insects turn up in your dreams, always use the symbol exercises in Chapter Five to work out what these creatures specifically mean to you, as they will contain potent messages for you. One way is to simply consider the natural behaviour of the creature that has turned up and relate this to your dream and your life. For example, if a wolf shows up in your dream, you know it's a hunter. Are you being hunted or doing the hunting in your dream? How does that relate to your current life?

Here are some examples of animal dreams:

* *'I am aware that the lion is loose. I am afraid, knowing the lion will kill me, but my self-preservation is high. I can't actually see the lion, but I can hear and feel its presence.'* Wild beasts such as lions tap into our primal animal urges. Where is this dreamer not accepting and owning their power to be 'king of the jungle'?

* *'A dog is biting my hand and I can't get free. People are around but they won't help.'* 'Biting the hand that feeds it' – where is this dreamer sabotaging herself? She needs to start taking responsibility for herself rather than playing the victim to set herself free.

* *'I was sitting on top of a very high grey filing cabinet and looking through a photo book of animals. The photo I remember was of a giraffe. Just its head was in the photo and there was a huge spider in its mouth. But the spider seemed to have too many legs and I remember thinking, "That doesn't make sense, giraffes only eat leaves."'* The two most important elements of a giraffe are its neck and head – it has keen eyesight and is far-sighted. What is it about the future and the way ahead that this dreamer needs to focus on? The spider represents industry, connection and in metaphysical terms a moment of destiny. Whatever's about to occur in this dreamer's life is

a sliding-doors moment. Where does the dreamer need to ingest the importance of the changes coming up?

Birds are the species that connect us with the heavens above. We already know that a primary human desire is to fly and be free, so birds in our dreams tend to represent messages from the Higher Self, although again always look at the specific characteristics of the bird that turns up to get more details of the type of message being conveyed.

Insects are something we all have to share space on the planet with, so they'll inevitably appear in our dreams. Each type of insect has its own set of characteristics. However, as a rule, insects appear in dreams much as they show up in life: as sources of minor irritation or annoyance with people or situations. At this stage it is only a minor irritation, but, left unchecked, insects can grow quickly, swell to vast numbers and be harbingers of disease.

When insects appear in a dream the message is often work related, as most insects are creatures of industry – bees, ants, spiders, locusts, etc. In their positive aspect they can be asking you to look at where you can increase collaboration and where relationship building and teamwork will really help you. Have you been isolating yourself too much lately or thinking you have to do everything yourself?

Obviously, if you have a phobia regarding a particular insect and it appears in a frightening manner, then it is literally your fear of that creature surfacing and the dream will be suggesting you look at a more obvious fear in your current life that you haven't dealt with.

Here's an example of an insect dream:

I was lying down chatting to someone when a couple of people ran past being chased by a swarm of bees. The bees landed on me. It was a relatively small swarm, I was not totally covered and I was able to breathe. I sat as still as possible until all the bees flew away. I remember feeling very calm and knowing that I must keep still. As the last few bees flew away there was a small bubble of honey attached to each one. I was not stung...

This is a positive insect dream: the bees are pollinating the dreamer's life. Where can she be still and let success percolate and come to her rather than chasing after it?

Falling, Feeling Trapped, Getting Lost

Again, these dreams come as a result of our universal human vulnerabilities. The world can be a scary place at times and this will inevitably be reflected in dreamtime.

✳ *'I'm trapped in a building and can't get out.'* What aspect of the self is this dreamer trapped by? How can she set herself free? What in her character is trapping her?

Dreams of falling are interesting, because as well as being a danger, falling is in our language: we fall asleep, we fall in love, we fall for people, we fall over ourselves, we fall out, etc. Look in these areas when a falling dream occurs.

I'm walking on a street – walking normally, not running, not afraid, just walking – and then suddenly I'm starting to fall down and then I feel afraid that I will hurt myself, hurt my head, but before I'm down a pillow pops up under my head and I'm just falling on that without hurting myself.

This dreamer is facing her fears and is assured a soft landing. Her dreaming mind is reassuring her that she has all the resources she needs to be safe.

Here's how discussing and working with a dream of this nature can resolve it:

*I'm standing on a huge cliff, looking down. I can see
a small beach at the bottom and the sea. I'm thinking:
'That's it! If I ever commit suicide, I'll make sure it's a
big drop like this one, so that I'll be sure to die and not
just cripple myself. Hang on a minute, though – what if,
because it's such a big drop, I change my mind halfway
down?' So I don't jump.*

The dreamer was feeling unable to take a leap in his career.
After he reported this dream, he made significant steps
forward in his life, as evidenced by a subsequent dream:

*I am walking on the moon with my parents. The ground
looks as though it is made of volcanic white cardboard. All
of a sudden I look down and I can see the Earth, so I think,
'Hey, that's a brilliant opportunity' and I jump! I come down
through space, through the atmosphere, through skyscrapers
and then blackness. I land softly, stretch and keep on walking.
It feels incredible.*

Houses, Buildings, Dwellings

A structure in which to take shelter has been a human
requirement for survival ever since we were cave dwellers.
Buildings of all kinds frequently appear in dreams.
Metaphysically speaking, homes in particular are symbolic of
our psyche.

New rooms in houses are generally a positive sign,
meaning new aspects of yourself are opening up. You may
have a dream of this nature as you work through this book,
unlocking doors into your inner world. The more we know
our dreams, the more we open up to a greater knowledge of
ourselves. A woman whose house I healed recently heralded
in the changes by dreaming of finding two new rooms in her

home she'd never seen. Her unconscious was ahead of the game, preparing her to accept greater understanding of herself now that change was afoot.

If buildings appear in a dream or the dream takes place in a building, ask yourself where the action is taking place. Is it in the kitchen, the 'heart of the home', or perhaps the 'living' room? The basement tends to represent the unconscious and the past. The ground-floor rooms are our conscious and everyday affairs, the bedrooms our inner selves and secret desires, and the attic our Higher Self and the future. Now you know what part of your life the action relates to, ask what part of your psyche needs to develop in alignment with the dream messages you've received.

Dreams of Death

Dreams of death are extremely common and do not mean you're about to die. I've had lots of dreams about dying and I'm still here. Dreams of death are actually about transformation and rebirth. They're about what you need to get rid of, what is no longer serving you. If death is showing up in your dream, some aspect of the self needs to die in order for you to make progress. You can use any of the dream techniques in this book to find out more or ask your dream symbol(s)/character(s) the following questions to find out what you need to let go of:

* Why are you killing me?
* Why am I killing you? What do you represent?
* What part of me are you trying to kill off?
* Why are you making me afraid?

I have really horrible dreams in which someone is trying to kill me or I'm trying to kill someone so they don't kill me first. I have these dreams a few times a week...

What does the dreamer need to 'kill off' in her life that she is not yet prepared to let go of?

Dreams about killing and death may sound alarming, but the emotion of a dream is vital. If I'm asking about a dream I'll always enquire about what people felt in it. You could have two people dreaming of killing and one dreamer having no feelings about it and the other being incredibly distraught. That is indicative of what is going on in their unconscious processing. Killing somebody in a dream is most likely to be a metaphor of needing to kill something off in yourself. The person who doesn't have any emotional attachment to that is probably in the process of already doing it, whereas the person who is experiencing horror at the very thought of killing somebody and wakes up traumatized is having far more resistance to the changes that they need to make in their life. Feelings in dreams tell us everything we need to know. They're vital emotional barometers.

Engaging with our dreams of death also helps prepare us for death. Many of our fears come from an underlying fear of death. Yes, our physical body will disappear, but our spirit will remain and we can choose our death in a far more conscious manner than most of us do today. Certain highly accomplished shamans and other 'holy' figures plan their death with as much care as their life. Yet we, for the most part, ignore death on every level until we can't ignore it. It happens, out of the blue, a complete surprise, or we hang on, clinging to a half life, a living death, such is our desperation not to let go. If we pay attention to our dreams, however, we connect with our true selves and death is no longer fearful but simply a gateway to the next great adventure.

Interpreting 'Problem' Dreams

Interpreting a dream, of whatever nature, gets easier with practice. At first you may only get the odd insight or struggle to make the connections, but once you activate your dreaming attention, the part that recognizes you are searching for meaning, you unlock the dreaming floodgates.

Here are some great questions to help you solve any dream:

Ten Questions to Solve Problem Dreams

1. What is the problem presented in the dream?
2. How is that a problem?
3. What would have to happen to resolve the problem presented in the dream?
4. If I'd already found a simple solution to this dream, what would it be?
5. What would I like to have happen as a result of resolving this problem?
6. What will that do for me? How will it serve me?
7. What have I learned from that dream? What would be a better lesson?
8. Where do I face these dream challenges in my current life?
9. What action do I need to take to stop them recurring?
10. And what do I know now?

Prophetic, Precognitive and Psychic Dreams

These are an extraordinarily common phenomenon. I'm sure you've had at least one of them yourself.

For most of us, dreams where we've known of a future event before it occurred tend to fall within two broad categories: they either relate to people we have a high emotional connection to, such as partners or family members, or they relate to large-scale global events. Here are some examples of the former type:

My prophetic dreams began when I gave birth to my daughter. All my dreams started coming then. I dreamed that my friend was standing next to a bed and crying and crying. When I woke, I said to my husband, 'Oh God, something's happened to my friend. I need to ring her.' I rang her and left a message and I said, 'I don't know why you were crying or what the problem is, but call me and tell me you're OK.' She called me later that day and said, 'Oh God, my dad died last night.' She was in America and had been next to his bed crying. I hadn't known her dad was sick. I hadn't even known she was in America.

Another time I dreamed there was a baby and it was putting its hand, slicing its hand, through its mother's stomach, as if it was coming out of the stomach. I woke up and said to my husband, 'Somebody's baby is going to be born by C-section,' and then I got a phone call and my sister in Spain had had a Caesarean that afternoon.

When the prophetic dreams come there's usually something odd happening, something that I remember, something that the minute I wake up I immediately think I must act on. Something in my subconscious tells me I need to act on it, whereas other times nothing happens. The prophetic dreams are always around birth and death.

This dreamer's last comments are key. Dreams of a precognitive nature concerning loved ones do seem to be predominantly around big life-changing events and do seem to have a different quality to the observant dreamer. Of course that quality is going to be different for each of us and you'll only really know it by observing the nature of your own dreams. Nevertheless, there are common elements. Often a call to action is present, as mentioned above, and a certain brightness or particular clarity is common, as are unusual characters or events that really stay with you long after the dream is over.

There are endless examples of the other type of precognitive dream, that relating to major tragic events such as the Twin Towers disaster and the Boxing Day tsunami in

2004. With what we now understand about time, perhaps these phenomena are more easily explained.

Another way of viewing these predictive capabilities is understanding that our unconscious always knows before our conscious mind what's on the way because it has more sensors available for picking up external data and also has a hotline to the Higher Self, which our conscious mind doesn't. We all live in this primordial energy soup where subtle forms of data are constantly available. Days before the Boxing Day tsunami, the energy of that earthquake was already building in the atmosphere. Similarly, with 9/11, it was in people's consciousness and being planned way before it happened.

Consider, too, that each of us during our lifetime probably has at least one tidal-wave dream and one aeroplane-disaster dream. If we confine ourselves to just two billion people and extrapolate the statistics on this, the night before the Boxing Day tsunami there were a minimum of 60,000 such dreams, as there have been every night before and since. That tends to put predictive dreams back in perspective. This is not to dismiss them but rather to suggest that, as with all dreams, they're predominantly signifiers of self. This is illustrated in this next dream:

Over the past couple of years there have been four plane crashes that have been featured on the news. I have dreamed about them all a week or two prior to them occurring. Each time I have seen the plane coming down, I haven't seen the airline and I haven't seen the people, just the plane coming down and then the actual crash. I wake as soon as it's happened. I've put it down to coincidence, but after dreaming about the most recent one I'm starting to feel a bit odd about it all.

Whilst acknowledging the predictive element of this woman's dream, in my response I focused on the personal. I asked whether her life had been periods of growth and development followed by major crashes, i.e. a bit of a roller-coaster ride. Maybe this dream was her unconscious warning her about gaining balance and stability in her life to stop the recurrence of crashing and burning each time she tried to succeed. This was the response I received:

Thank you so much for suggesting the reasons for my dreams. In fact, they're spot on. Succeeding, then crashing is the order of the day, I'm afraid, and has been for quite a while! Not only in my career but relationship-wise too; 'roller coaster' is a perfect description of my life!

The lesson we all need to take from this is that whatever else dreams are, ultimately they're personal, and we can only work meaningfully with them at that level.

Another dream I was sent related to a dreamer who needed to let go of her emotional attachment to the past. Her unconscious very helpfully told her straight to the point it was time to let go:

On 22 May 2009 I dreamed about a man I had once loved and had not seen or heard from in four years. Clearly I had not let go properly and I had a dream that he got married (the full dream was we were hanging out and he disappeared, I searched and searched and then he came out of a church with someone else). I discovered later that he had indeed got married and it had been on 22 May!

If you're troubled by precognitive dreams in any way, remember this key point: the future is not fixed. By knowing it, we can change it. It's our assumptions, stories and beliefs that create our tomorrows; if we change those, we'll change our future.

Lucid Dreams

We can't leave this chapter without a brief word on lucid
dreaming, as most of us have had at least one experience of
this. A lucid dream is when you know that you're dreaming in
the dream. You can then consciously direct the dream action.
In a sense, this is what we do with daydreaming. A daydream
is a kind of lucid dream, particularly if we set our imagination
free, enabling it to contemplate the unlimited possibilities that
exist.

Shamans are masters in the art of lucid dreaming, as are
the Tibetan yogis. They categorize the art of dreaming further.
For them it is possible to tell the difference between an
ordinary dream and a journey to another dimension. There is,
according to Don Juan, the nagual shaman who taught Carlos
Castaneda, an easy way to distinguish between ordinary
dreams and other dimensions, and that is by seeing the energy.
Ordinary dreams are energetically inert, they have no aura,
whereas beings in other dimensions have energetic imprints
that can be perceived if you have developed your own energy
body enough to see them properly.

To improve the lucidity of your dreams, you need to
practise. One way is every time you walk through a doorway,
look at both sides of your hands and ask, 'Is this a dream?'
It instils the behaviour and at some point you will find your
hand looks different and you'll know you're dreaming.

That's when it gets exciting, as you are now master of your
dreams. If you want to fly, you can, learn a new skill, you
can. You're in the fantastical make-believe world of dreams,
where you can make anything happen. Lucid dreams give you
enormous freedom, as you have none of the normal physical
restrictions of being human. It's an exhilarating feeling. You
can also face and conquer nightmares, as this dreamer did:

*For years as a child growing up I had a recurring dream of a
tidal wave coming after me. In the dream I was running and*

running. It was horrible and happened virtually every night. Then in my twenties I dreamed the same dream again and I knew I was dreaming. I stood on the shore and turned and looked at the tidal wave and it just stopped moving. It was way up high, like a mountain, and it was beautiful actually. It froze and I just looked at it. I stood looking at it for a long time and I never got the dream again.

We can all achieve this possibility but in my experience some people are more predisposed to be able to do it at will than others. I've practised a lot and although I get a high proportion of lucid dreams I can't yet decide to have one at will, though some people can.

An in-depth discussion of lucid dreaming is beyond the scope of this book, but if you do want to learn more I'd recommend the work of Steven Laberge, developer of the MILD technique, the well-known induction for lucid dreaming.

CHAPTER NINE

Your New Best Friends

Healing Dreams

*'In my dream, the Angel shrugged and said,
"If we fail this time, it will be a failure of
imagination." And then she placed the world
gently in the palm of my hand.'*
Erica Jong

In the ancient world, before we lost the art of dreaming,
night-time whisperings were considered important in terms
of healing. Both Hippocrates, the father of modern medicine,
and his contemporary Socrates wrote about the potential
healing power of dreams. Aristotle believed that they could
be signs of physical conditions within the body. He argued
against them as a source of divine inspiration and argued for
them as a pictorial response to internal physical feelings and
sensations. The Greek physician Galen was a true believer in
the power of dreams as healing messengers to the extent that
he apparently undertook medical procedures based on the
results of his dream interpretation, whilst Plato considered
the liver the house of dreams and believed it gave rise to
prophetic dreams.

On one level all dreams are healing dreams, as they're
all feedback loops from our unconscious to our conscious,

letting us know what's going on. At the very least they keep us mentally healthy and are healing in and of themselves, even if we don't consciously remember them. In a recent study, students who were awakened at the beginning of each dream period but still allowed their eight hours of sleep all experienced loss of concentration, irritability, hallucinations and signs of psychosis after only three days. When finally allowed their dream sleep, their brains made up for lost time by greatly increasing the percentage of sleep spent in the REM stage.

Health and Healing

Let's begin our look at healing dreams by defining healing or health. This is a state of well-being or feeling good. In the same way, ill health is about feeling bad. Health is not a thing – we can't put it in a wheelbarrow – yet we talk about having health or not having it, as though we could do exactly that.

Similarly, most healing practices talk about getting rid of illness as if it were a thing. I'd like us to consider a model of the world where in fact health and illness are forms of behaviour. Remember our body, governed by the unconscious mind, is always moving towards pleasure. Sometimes, though, that pleasure could look like pain! The body is not able to solve the issue, because somehow the conscious mind is not cooperating, so the body may produce an illness, for example in an attempt to solve a problem. If, say, you hate your job and are constantly saying to yourself and/or others, 'I'm sick of this job,' the unconscious mind listens and obligingly responds by giving you the flu, and hence time away from work. From the perspective of the unconscious mind, this is the most pleasurable of the available choices based on the information it is being fed from you, i.e. 'I'm sick of this job.'

So feelings and thoughts create behaviour that creates illness. Unhelpful behaviour will also lead to stress, and stress, as we know, increasingly interferes with the body's healthy functioning.

Ongoing tension and stress also get in the way of healing. The more effectively we can deal with the tension, the more quickly we can heal. Any cure or healing method that relieves tension creates the space for healing to take place automatically. Which demonstrates why practices such as yoga, meditation, acupuncture and *tai chi* are so effective for healing – they all focus on releasing cellular stress. Relieving tension is key, hence the emphasis in this book on relaxation and relieving negative dream emotions, as these are sources of tension in the body.

Here's a practice to resolve any tension felt in the physical body as a result of dream imagery or memory. You can use it to work on pain and stress in your waking reality too.

SELF-HEALING DREAM BREATHING

✱ Sit and relax. Think about what the dream has left you with in your body. Is it pain, stress, tension, fever? Where can you feel it in your physical body?

✱ When you think of that problem, what kind of place in the world would hold the perfect healing energy for you right now? Would it be a peaceful, cooling lake for a fever, a sacred power spot for a loss of power, an oak tree to give strength, the healing well at Lourdes? Wherever feels perfect for you, direct your mind to that spot now.

✱ Now focus on your breathing... Inhale, through your nose, the energy from that perfect place you've created in your mind and exhale, through your nose, into your body through your belly. If you put your mind there, and wait, the breath will naturally relax and follow.

✱ Do this quietly for a few breaths, allowing the breath to breathe the body...

✳ Now take your awareness to the problem in your body. Continue to inhale from the healing image and exhale the breath into that place … softly … naturally.

✳ Embrace the tension or pain and allow it to dissolve and relax. No judgement, no pressure … just let go a little more with each out-breath, allowing the tension to melt away.

✳ Continue softening and breathing until the tension or pain has released.

If we understand the body–mind relationship as a highly energized two-way communication highway, then it becomes easier to see how we can heal through building rapport between the conscious and the unconscious mind.

We've all heard of the placebo effect where people are given a sugar pill but told it is a healing medicine and they heal at the same rate or even faster than the people given the actual medicine. I've seen the remarkable effect of this first hand as a nurse. Post-operative analgesics are potent and highly addictive for some people. Occasionally a patient would develop a dependency very quickly and the doctor would prescribe a placebo injection rather than the opiate. The patient *believing* they were getting the analgesic would soon be pain free. What's doing the healing in these cases? Belief, personal assumptions, positive emotions and good communication between all parts of the mind.

To speed up healing we need therefore to harmonize the relationship between our mind and body. When we view the world in a certain way, it becomes easier. Many shamans have a holistic view and specialize in placebos, or what has been termed sympathetic magic. Often they will complete a healing by giving the client a task to do, ostensibly to complete their work but in reality to keep them focused on their own healing. Completion of the task by the client gives conscious permission to their unconscious to carry out the required healing. The shaman's objective is the healing and that's more important than the method, whereas to most doctors it's the method that counts. These different assumptions lead to the different healing models that exist in our world today. Most shamans would consider that all illness is in the mind, which is why they pay more attention to their dreams than we do. For them, dreams are a great source of information as to what is producing the illness.

Ultimately, I believe all healing comes from within, not the doctor or the shaman or the pills. Our bodies are designed to heal themselves naturally and our dreams help us unlock what we need to resolve in order to heal.

Engaging with Healing Dreams

The benefit of healing dreams does depend on our ability to understand their meaning. But dreams can alert us to something specifically related to health. There's masses of anecdotal evidence of this. A client of mine, for example, dreamed of a hand biting his bottom lip. When he awoke, he could still feel the dream imprint on the lip and actually checked in the mirror and noticed that he had badly receding gums on the two teeth the dream hand had been pointing to. As a result, he went to the dentist and did require treatment.

Teeth seem to feature in dreams in particular, but you need to use your discretion in terms of the meaning. Losing teeth is a very common dream, as we discovered in Chapter Eight. As we know, this is a rite-of-passage dream, not about dental health but about leaving something old behind and moving into something new. I had a vivid dream of losing my teeth whilst writing this book. I could see immediately how that related to my current life situation, so I didn't book a dentist's appointment. That's the key to knowing. Check in with the feel of the dream first and see it if relates to your life. If it feels at odds with what's happening to you or starts to recur, or your dreams start to get progressively more nightmarish, then probably something needs investigating further.

Often the dreaming mind is faster at picking up problems than the physical body is at creating the symptoms, which presents another issue. If, for example, you dream you have cancer eating away at some part of your body but when you go for tests nothing is picked up, it could simply be that it has not developed fully in the body yet. I've learned to trust dream messages implicitly, as I have always seen them manifest truthfully. There are endless examples of people who have had a dream pertaining to a symptom that was not yet physically present, or perhaps more accurately not yet consciously apparent, that did later manifest.

If we can engage in our dreams in a meaningful way, then we can extract meaningful information from them and work with them in order to be able to heal any physical ailments within the dream process. The trick, of course, is recognizing or understanding when such a message appears, as dreams are always multi-layered and multi-faceted in their meaning. This is where the exercises in this book really help. They are designed to allow you to get clarity on what is and what is not relevant about any particular dream you have.

Here's a dreamer who takes notice of her healing dream messages after years of getting healing messages from her horses:

A few months ago I dreamed of a chestnut horse. I had the feeling that somehow this horse would be very important in my life and I should take notice of it in some way. All I could see in the dream was a chestnut-coloured mane in front of me. At the time I didn't know any chestnut-coloured horses.

A few weeks later I was asked to ride a chestnut horse for someone. I turned up to ride not knowing anything about the horse. I immediately recalled my dream but got on with the riding.

*Now every time I ride this horse (and I have ridden for
years without any problems) I have gotten cystitis and been
in agony a few days later and a course of antibiotics has
followed each time. A month ago I got a kidney infection after
leaving the trip to the doc's for too long and ended up having
a week off work. During that week I did a lot of thinking and
decided it was time to pursue my dream of coaching with
horses and I handed in my notice at work. Despite seven days
of very strong antibiotics not working, the infection was gone
almost immediately I'd made the decision.*

I do appreciate this is perhaps the most difficult dreaming area
to be certain of without the benefit of hindsight. It requires
considerable trust in yourself and possibly persistence on
your part if the dream does give clear indication of an issue.
Therefore the exercises in this chapter are designed to get
clarity around your dream first and then to work with your
healing on an energetic basis, hopefully solving the problem
before it becomes one.

One way to find out more is simply to ask for a dream on
the matter. If you're sick, ask for a dream about how you
can help your healing most and see what shows up. (There is
more detailed information on how to set up a creative-solution
dream in Chapter Eleven.)

Any dream that troubles us in some way, either through its
inexplicable nature or its overwhelming emotions, will be a
call from our unconscious that healing is required on some
level. And remember, healing is holistic – it can affect any
level of our being. It doesn't have to be physical, it can be
emotional, spiritual and psychological, as this deeply moving
dream story from world-renowned guitarist Martin Taylor
illustrates:

*My son died when he was 21. He took his own life. His
short life was dedicated to riding horses. He was a brilliant*

horseman. We come from a Gypsy family and horses and music are in our blood.

I became overwhelmed with grief and I had to stop my work as a professional musician and go home to my family. I spent four weeks in bed trying to recover from the pain.

Sometimes during that time I would talk to my wife in a language that she couldn't understand. She wrote a lot of my ramblings down and showed them to me later. Some of it I recognized as the Romany language, even though I don't know the language that well. The rest was a strange language that was later identified as an ancient dialect spoken many years ago in southern Italy. I have no connection with Italy.

During those dark days, for the first time in my life there was no music going on in my head, just a dark silence.

The turning point was when I had a dream where the music started to play again and the most familiar song came to me. I played it on my guitar and the words came into my head:

> You rode a horse like a king and you sang like an angel,
> You're my Romany chavo [boy], my dear Gypsy boy.

I'm a guitarist, not a lyricist, so I handed the song to my friend, the great folk musician Martin Simpson, and he finished it for me. He knew my son and knew the story. I called it 'One Day' and he recorded it on his album True Stories.

There's something about that song that affects people on a very deep level. I don't know where it came from, but it has been a big part of my healing process.

Waking Dreams

We don't only have healing dreams when we're asleep. We can use waking dreams or visualizations to heal ourselves in many wonderful ways.

Visualization has been used by top athletes to improve their performance for many years. Those athletes that visualize running the entire race, as well as winning it repeatedly, do far better than those that just visualize the end result of winning.

This is an important distinction and one that's relevant for all imagination exercises, including healing visualizations. The mind cannot distinguish between reality and what is vividly imagined. Think of squeezing a fresh ripe lemon – immediately your mouth is salivating. This is the mind–body connection. As a result, when you do the healing visualizations that follow, it is about feeling healing taking place in your physical body as you take the journey. It is as important to feel the process of healing occurring at the cellular level within the body as it is to see the picture in your mind of yourself completely well and healthy.

Trust your dreams and your ability to heal. Every thought, every feeling, every action is a message to your immune system – make it a life-affirming one.

Remembering what you know about the power of the mind, you can use your active imagination to work with the dream imagery to resolve the issue it's showing you. This is akin to energy medicine and absolutely works, as everything is ultimately energy.

Here's a simple healing journey that can be done at any time of day or night. It takes you on a journey to a healing garden, to a special healing sanctuary. If I'm feeling out of sorts I will often travel to my healing garden as I'm drifting off to sleep and spend the night in my sanctuary.

HEALING SANCTUARY JOURNEY

You can use this process on its own as a healing journey or you can take an unresolved dream or problem into the garden with you for resolution.

Relax and get comfortable, either sitting or lying down. Let your mind wander and find yourself in a garden ... the garden of your mind.

Spend a few moments getting acquainted with it. Look around... Feel what you feel... See what you see... Hear what you hear ... and notice what you notice. What's the weather like in your garden? Is the garden large or small? Does it have boundaries? Are there others in the garden with you? Whatever shows up is perfect for you. This is your mindscape. It is perfectly safe and completely secure...

Remember that now as you take a deep, slow breath in and out through your nose and totally relax ... now. That's right ... and even deeper than that ... relax.

Somewhere in this garden is a healing sanctuary perfectly and beautifully designed just for you. Go there now... Let your awareness allow it to appear before you... That's right.

Explore this sanctuary... What makes it perfect for you? Is it the colours? The design? The music? The scents? Or something else entirely? What would make it even more perfect for you right now? Remember this is your mindscape to play with as you will. Perhaps you could ask for a spirit doctor to lend an opinion or get a soothing head massage... Whatever you desire for your healing is here, ready, waiting for you. Is there a certain food you need, or a medicine? Then create it – the possibilities are limited only by your imagination. Let yours be free now to allow the right healing environment for you... That's right. Just relax and enjoy your healing sanctuary.... Remember you are free to change it at will.

If there is an issue or dream you wish to work on, bring it to mind now and ask for the solution to appear ... and trust that it will as you continue to relax in your space of peace...

Continue for as long as you feel comfortable ... and when you feel complete, wiggle your toes and fingers, clench your fists, stretch your arms above your head and then bring them down, relaxing your hands, and open your eyes fully back in the room you're sitting in.

Spend some time reflecting on your journey and its insights. Pay particular heed to any foods or medicines that appeared. You may have received some symbols you need to understand further using the processes you learned earlier.

In light of the new information received, what action could you take now in your life to begin resolving the presenting problem?

I am ... Whatever Is in my Dream

This next dream process, based on Gestalt therapy, is good to use on any dream and is particularly useful for potential healing dreams. Working on the assumption that all elements in a dream are part of Me, Inc., we're simply going to allow the pertinent element in your dream to have its say. Here's an example from a workshop to illustrate the technique:

My recurring dream comes in slightly different versions, but basically I'm either on a beach or I'm standing on sand and this is the linking thing: there are always massive amounts of sand.

The dreamer used the technique to allow the sand to have its say:

✱ *'Relax. If it makes it easier, close your eyes. Just be the sand now, you are actually the sand in your dream. I want*

*you to say, "I am the sand," and talk as the sand, out loud.
Say anything that comes to you. It doesn't matter how silly or
ridiculous it sounds, it's just a game we're playing.'*

✳ *'I am the sand. I am wet – the tidewater has moved away,
leaving me wet. When people walk across me they sink in.
They're wearing the wrong shoes to cross me. It's dull and
boring being the sand. I'm not doing anything, nothing is
happening, I'm just existing. I can see a lot of people but
they're all in the distance. There is nobody actually on me.
I feel ignored. Nobody's bothered to be here, they're all too
busy getting on with everything.'*

✳ *'And the learning...?'*

✳ *'Before today, I thought the underlying problem was
just anxiety. But now I realize my issues with my friends are
massively important to me. I feel I'm not getting certain
things right and I need to approach these in a different way.
It's not that my whole life is bad, but because I value friends
so strongly and that's the part of my life that's not working,
I'm really worrying about it.'*

You can speak from any aspect in your dream by simply
relaxing and putting your awareness into that object and
speaking from its perspective. Then you are hearing its point
of view, which of course ultimately is just another point
of view you hold yourself somewhere about something or
someone.

At the end of the exercise always reflect the conversation
back to yourself, as the dreamer bravely did above. This is
how we heal – by recognizing and facing our 'stuff'. You may
like to record your session aloud and play it back to yourself.
Often hearing it repeated in that way highlights the meaning
for you and you get that 'Aha!' moment as it reveals itself.

Now you know what the dream means, you need to
consider how you can implement positive changes in your

life. Dreams are only useful if we bother to do something about them. For example, our dreamer above needs to take steps towards improving her friendships because they are what's important to her.

Physical Symptoms

Dreams relating to an area of the physical body in some way are definitely worth investigating if the dream is overtly negative. Do this by checking your lifestyle habits first. Have you been neglecting yourself of late? Missing out on sleep? Been ill? Or feel out of sorts generally? Dreams of this nature are often recurring, so before pursuing the issue check your dream journal for recurrences.

Sometimes healing dreams are literal – you may get a doctor turn up in your dream, operating or pointing to an area of your body. Our unconscious works far faster than our conscious mind in relation to the physical body.

A woman on TV recently kept dreaming that she had a brain haemorrhage and then had one in real life. She didn't act on these very literal dreams, but luckily she survived. Perhaps just the fact that she'd had the dream somehow lessened the impact of the real event. She'd repeatedly dreamed the event so when it actually occurred her physiology was somehow more prepared for it.

I had a similar experience when I dreamed that I had a fatal accident in a red car that hit a lorry. When the accident subsequently happened in real life, the only reason I believe it wasn't fatal was that the dream had prepared me somehow for the real event. Funnily enough, as I hit the lorry I remember thinking, 'Oh, this is my dream,' and I relaxed completely. It was the weirdest sensation. The car was a total write-off and I had to be helped from the wreckage, yet I walked away without a scratch. I'm convinced that dream saved me, despite not fully understanding the mechanism of how it did that.

Early-warning dreams about accidents and physical conditions do tend to have a particular quality, I think. In my research I've discovered there is something about these dreams that is slightly different from other dreams. It's hard to explain, but there is something in your psyche that tells you that these dreams are something to do with your physical self. They tend to be vivid dreams that stay with you long afterwards. If you ever get a hunch or an odd feeling about a dream like this, please follow it up. Your unconscious truly is your best friend and will always send you messages that you need to hear. Unlocking these, using the techniques in this book, will connect you to your healing power.

Here's an account of one woman's early dream warning:

On 20 February 2000 I dreamed that my brother had liver cancer. He had been for X-rays and he had 'buttons' on his liver and it was all a sort of marmalade colour.

I went on to dream that I was on a train to Penzance with lots of people that I knew. I left my seat and when I returned a woman was sitting there and would not move. She was reading my letters and doing my sewing. Eventually she took my jar of Colman's seedy mustard. A little was left in the bottom and she added milk because she thought it was too thick. I grabbed it, shook it and threw it all over her, and then she moved.

We had to change trains later and then had to walk through a wilderness and past beautiful flowerbeds. I was picking the flowers and the others all copied me, picking the delphiniums, etc.

When we arrived at the station, which was a stately home, the woman in the train seat had called the plain-clothes police, but they were not real police officers.

In 2004 I was diagnosed with primary breast cancer and in 2008 I was diagnosed with secondary cancer in my liver and all of my bones. I had always remembered that dream and wondered about the connection.

Although at first glance this may seem a difficult dream to interpret, there is a massive amount of relevant information contained within it if you know about this woman's life and her associations. This is why we always need to be working closely with our own dreams – they're the only ones we can truly understand.

This dreamer was not close to her brother; she described their relationship as 'distant' – exactly the same relationship she had with the liver cancer at the time of this dream. It was not yet physically showing up. Her brother might have been distant but she nevertheless has a blood relationship with him and the liver is the purifier of the blood in the body and relates to family issues in metaphysical medicine. We already know from our dream symbols that a train represents our way of journeying through life. A train to Penzance conjures up a long journey, controlled by others, which is similar to undergoing prolonged cancer treatment. This dreamer's place on the journey (her seat) was taken by an unpleasant woman who took over her life, just as the breast cancer subsequently interrupted, then took over, her life. Her attempts to fight back have had limited success (throwing the mustard), but she can create time for herself by changing direction in life (changing trains) and spending more time smelling the roses, although the wilderness suggests a period of darkness and confusion. When she tries to continue her journey, at the instigation of the unpleasant woman the plain-clothes cops who aren't real thwart her. In this part we can see where the dreamer is in denial: her conscious mind doesn't yet believe in the danger she's in. The police, normally viewed as a cause for alarm and attention, are seen as unreal. Their identity is also hidden, just as the seriousness of the cancer was, at the time of this dream, hidden from the dreamer.

Anxiety Dreams

Anxiety dreams are common. They tend to be ones about being chased, being trapped, being exposed and running away.

This is our body's way of dealing with the stress in our lives. We can deal with such dreams relatively simply by addressing the issue highlighted in them. Where are we feeling trapped, overwhelmed, fearful, etc. in our life? Do we need to change our job? What adjustments do we need to make to resolve this anxiety?

If you have an anxiety dream like this, it's telling you what's out of balance. Work with it to get yourself back in balance. If you do that, the dream will disappear – simple as that.

A great way to relieve tension and anxiety in the body, either from dreams or just generally, is to use the meditation technique below. I originally learned this way of working with tension when I certified as an endorphination trainer with William Bloom, author of *The Endorphin Effect*. This particular exercise is based on the Taoist tradition of the inner smile. Its power lies in the mind–body connection. If you'd like to learn more of these techniques I'd highly recommend reading William's book.

HOW TO ENDORPHINATE – THE INNER SMILE TECHNIQUE

This exercise programs you to send the right messages to your body so that the tissues start to relax and open and release endorphins (happy hormones).

You can be sitting or lying down and when you're practised at it you can even do it standing up. It's my favourite way of passing time in queues at the supermarket or the bank (with my eyes open!).

Take your time to relax and feel every step of the process.

* Close your eyes and lower your eyelids and your chin.

* Lower your chest and shoulders. Let your body drop and your shoulders slump. Drop into yourself.

* Feel your buttocks, thighs, knees, feet on the floor.

* Become aware that you're attached to this spinning planet. Feel the gravitational pull of the hot molten centre of the Earth pulling you into it. It's very comforting for us to feel that sensation.

* Relax and soften your stomach.

* Take some deep, long, quiet, slow breaths into your stomach. Notice how your breath moves your chest and stomach.

* Soften your eyes and allow them to softly smile under the closed lids.

* Soften and relax your jaw.

* Focus on the world inside your skin. Become aware of any physical sensations occurring in your body.

* Adopt a compassionate, kind, loving attitude to the physical sensations, as though you were caring for a puppy or kitten or a sleeping baby you don't wish to wake. 'Hello, body, how're you doing today? You OK? Thanks for breathing, etc.'

* Allow any good sensation, no matter how subtle, to sink deeply into you like a sponge soaking up water.

* Let your heart open and melt.

* Do this with all the organs in the body with a kind loving attitude. Greet and smile into each organ.

* Become aware of any pain, tension or discomfort in your body. Relax and smile into it with this same loving kindness

* When you're ready, stretch and open your eyes and come back to an awareness of your surroundings.

Healing Dream Retreats

In the ancient world, as we already know, healing dreams were taken seriously and in Hellenic times dream temples were commonplace. They were dedicated to the Greek god of healing, Asklepios. If you were ill and the doctor could not help, you would muster your resources and embark on the long journey to a dream temple. On arrival, you would spend time preparing for your night in the *abaton*, or dream incubation chamber. Here you spent the night in anticipation of receiving a dream visit from the great god himself. He would either miraculously cure your ailment or offer advice on what you needed in order to heal. Only one night in the *abaton* per visit was allowed, therefore preparation was essential.

The temples were geared to enhancing the ability to dream. They were sited in places of great natural beauty. The mind was soothed with meditation practice and in-depth personal analysis. The body was cleansed through hydrotherapy treatments and detox diets. The soul was fed through music, poetry and theatre. Not until it was certain that you could sleep through the night and guarantee a healing dream would the therapeutes consider you ready for your 'once in a night-time' opportunity. Having probably used your life savings on this trip, you would certainly want to ensure you had a truly significant dream on the night you spent in the incubator. These dreams were considered so significant that the results were recorded on stone tablets that exist to this day. They bear witness to the fact that miraculous cures, spontaneous healings and solutions to problems arose effortlessly through the power of dreams.

Today we can recreate the essence of these dream-temple retreats by making the intention to lavish a little attention on ourselves and our dreams.

The ancient Greeks recognized our holistic nature. They treated the whole person, not just the dreaming mind. Here are a couple of adaptable dream techniques that I would highly recommend for healing any issues that occur in your life on any level.

Connecting to Asklepios, the God of Dream Healing

Remember our archetypes from Chapter Six? Well, we can consciously connect to archetypal energies as well as work with the ones already within us. In this next exercise we're going to connect to the archetypal healing energies of the Greek god of dream healing, Asklepios, asking him to work with us and give us healing messages through our dreams. The key to success in these endeavours is to trust your active imagination. Remember our power lies in our imagination and we already know that our brain cannot distinguish between something vividly imagined and something real.

This process allows you to combine the energies of the collective unconscious with your own personal story. Allowing yourself to believe in these universal energies assists you in receiving benefit from them. If your well-being is at stake, it has to be worth testing out, doesn't it?

MEDITATION ON ASKLEPIOS

Before sleeping, take a few minutes to relax, meditate and connect to Asklepios, who is traditionally seen as an elderly grey-bearded god. See this great being standing before you, facing you, fully focused on you. Acknowledge within yourself his healing power and great knowledge of dreams. He is a master Dream Whisperer.

Feel a beam of light energy coming from his forehead into your forehead and another beam of light from his heart to your heart.

After a few moments see him walk towards you, arms outstretched. Take him into your embrace and feel your energies merging. Tell your body to remember this feeling.

Pay particular attention to any dreams you receive.

Holiday Dream Quest

If you're concerned about health or have an existing condition you'd like to work with, then I would recommend the following dream retreat to focus your dreaming attention on the issue. I'm not suggesting that you should ignore modern medicine in favour of dream work; rather, I'm inviting you to use dreams in conjunction with or as an adjunct to regular medicine. Imagine a world where our modern medical professionals acknowledged the power of dreams. I wonder how much more successful our health system would be!

Holidays are a great time to play with dreams and discover their extraordinary benefits. We don't always have time during our busy working weeks to record and analyse the meaning of our dreams or ponder their hidden depths, but on holiday there is more time available. And for those of you who like puzzles, dreams are a gift indeed. What greater puzzle is there to solve than the secrets held within your own self?

On holiday, we also tend to remember more dreams. That's because we see holidays as a time to catch up and we allow ourselves to develop a more relaxed sleeping pattern. Therefore, we're likely to spend much longer periods in the REM dream sleep stage than usual. The alarm clock is off. We're able to wake naturally and to pause, recalling our dreams before the day starts.

This dream process was inspired by Pablo Friedlander, a great shaman and spiritual teacher from Argentina whom I have the honour of knowing and working with. His original teaching involved a much longer and more committed process. The following is perfect for modern, busy lives.

DREAM RETREAT

Take a journal, penlight and pens to bed with you, ready to record your dreams. I would do this process for a minimum of five nights and preferably longer. To make the process more effective I would suggest a cleansing diet for at least three days beforehand. No processed or fried foods, no meat, dairy, caffeine, sugar, drugs or alcohol. Eat plenty of fresh fruit and vegetables and wholegrains. Drink at least two litres of water daily. If your holiday facilities cater for it, take saunas and steam baths. If you're doing this retreat at home, a 20-minute sea salt or Epsom salt soak in the bath is helpful. This prepares your system for clear, unambiguous dreams.

Take a day or so to get into your holiday first to start to unwind, to let your mind soften and remember what it's like to slow down and take the time to ponder and reflect.

First, as always, set your intention. This is the rocket fuel that powers the information you ultimately receive. It keeps you on track and on purpose. So decide what you would like some insight into. Ask yourself the question: 'What would I most like to have happen as a result of engaging in this dream retreat?'

Always check your answer. Look at it and ask, 'How does that serve me? What does that give me/do for me?' This will crystallize what it is you are truly seeking.

When you finally have the key phrase or sentence summing up what you're going to program your dreaming mind for, write it in your dream journal with the date.

Before sleeping, take a shower, light a candle and spend some time meditating. The length of time is up to you, but at least five minutes would be beneficial. You can use any of the relaxation techniques suggested in this book to help you.

Go straight to bed, making sure the candle is out safely. Preferably lie on your back with your arms and legs uncrossed – at least whilst you're falling asleep, anyway. You may naturally move away from this position once asleep.

If you wake in the night with a dream, write it down immediately. If you wait until morning, it is 95 per cent likely to be lost.

In the morning, lie still. Listen intently as your dreams whisper to you and when you are ready, record as accurately and fully as possible all that you can recall. Remember it is best to always write dreams up in the present tense, as if the events are happening now, and it is important to include how the dream made you feel.

Repeat each night until you have finished the sequence you set yourself.

At the end of the sequence, find enough time that will allow you to read the sequence backwards uninterrupted. *Always* start with the last dream and read all the way through without interruption. If you are interrupted, you need to start the re-reading process again.

After your review, write one paragraph summing up, the recurrences, patterns, insights, connections and associations that are immediately apparent to you. This process will highlight your repeating patterns which, as we know, are those valuable diamonds we need to unearth to heal ourselves.

Once you have your dream themes, use any of the dream-interpretation techniques we've covered to unlock their meaning. Do not underestimate the power of this process or the wisdom of your dreaming mind.

To illustrate what can show up, here are some dreamers' recurring themes. None of these students had consciously realized that they had these repetitive elements running through their dreams and the associative behaviour running through their life.

All my dreams have a theme of having to climb rocky terrain and getting lost and struggling over rocks and mountains. I'd not noticed this before. And fear because I'm late. I think I'm being asked to look within myself and draw upon my experience with nature and it's very much about standing in my power, finding that part of myself.

I also have lots of dreams about being afraid of my husband. But it's not him, it's about being afraid of myself, the masculine part of myself.

I have lots of transportation dreams – boats, cars, buses, planes. There seems to be a theme of packing bags, a feeling of running away – movement, but real fear around movement.

I'm in the arms of my dream lover a lot and that feels divine. There does seem to be a lot of negative emotion from childhood being released. There's also a feeling of shame around simply not wanting to be around people.

And here's some feedback from a student who completed a 28-day dream retreat with me:

I now know that love is the most important virtue in my life and that I love to fly free of my limitations and I love to work and be in a magical realm and I now know this is what I was born to do and this is my life's purpose.

Dreams do not give us definitive answers to our problems; they offer possible solutions, inspiration and ideas. They will certainly comment on the decisions we make in either a positive or a negative way. But it is our conscious mind that holds the power of taking action, making choices based on the information and guidance that we receive from our dreaming mind.

Now let's get to grip with those deeper fears lurking within and shine the light on our nightmares.

CHAPTER TEN

Dealing with Fear

Nightmares and Night Terrors

'What if nothing exists and we're all in somebody's dream? Or, what's worse, what if only that fat guy in the third row exists?'
Woody Allen

No one likes having nightmares, but they can be a dreamer's greatest gift. Those dreams that cause us to awake screaming, heart pounding, those dreams that stay with us throughout the day, those are the unconscious mind's call to arms. It's the emergency hotline to the waking mind and it's asking you to pay attention now!

Nightmares keep us healthy; they are messengers of value. They shine their light on issues we are consciously choosing to ignore and force us to be prepared for associated issues in the waking world. They also alert us to potential problems in life that we're not willing to face. We can lie to ourselves, but we can't lie to our unconscious dreaming mind. And if we don't pay attention, the nightmares will repeat themselves until we do, often getting more nightmarish in the process. For example, a recent call I took on *The Wright Stuff* involved a woman dreaming that a ferocious lion came into a social setting and ate all her friends and family, leaving only her unharmed. She was having this dream four times a week because she was not facing up to the message it held for her, that message being that she needed to assert herself and face some confrontational issues with family members that she'd been avoiding due to fear of the repercussions.

Our dreams are excellent indicators of our repressions, unresolved traumas and unexpressed emotions. Whatever we've left undone gets stored away in our unconscious. Dreams do the emotional processing work for us, mostly outside our conscious awareness, and if we need to pay conscious attention and take action, our dreaming mind very kindly alerts us to this in the form of a nightmare or recurring dream. But once you've worked through these difficult or unresolved dreams you'll find that situation resolves in your life and you're able to move on without the need for lengthy therapy sessions or a breakdown!

Stress, traumatic experiences, emotional difficulties, certain drugs and illness can exacerbate the frequency and potency of nightmares, whilst certain barbiturates and antidepressants can lead to specific types of nightmare dreams. Some drugs depress dreaming function altogether and some lead to more hallucinogenic nightmares. If you're suffering nightmares because of post-traumatic stress syndrome (PTSS), you need professional help and although the exercises in this book will help you I would not advise doing them without a professional to assist you in the process. This condition can be relieved over time, but it takes longer than general everyday nightmares.

When we're stressed, we tend to sleep less deeply, less powerfully, and this has also been found to increase the number of nightmares. Illness changes our sleep cycles too and we tend to wake up more frequently. If we're running a high temperature, that can affect the chemicals in the brain and possibly produce more hallucinogenic dreams.

Whatever kind of nightmares you're having, viewing them as sources of valuable personal information will allow you to stay detached from the highly emotive elements long enough to be able to ferret out those gems of personal wisdom hidden within.

It's important to learn to relax rather than get tense around the content of any fear-based dream. Tension in the body causes fear and anxiety, but we can't actually produce those feelings if we're in a totally relaxed state.

Similarly, nightmare figures in our dreams are only scary whilst we're afraid and unwilling to face the fear that's showing up. Remember what we've learned about dreams so far: ultimately we're working in the realm of Me, Inc. – with dreams it's all personal! And what's really scarier, the repeating, escalating nightmares of your night-time or your refusal to make the life changes required to resolve the issue?

Let's begin with a simple exercise for being at peace with the enemy within.

DISCOVERING THE POSITIVE NATURE OF YOUR NIGHTMARES

✳ Choose a dream that is challenging for you to consider.

✳ Get into a relaxed state and focus on your heart.

✳ Imagine breathing in and out through your heart, inhaling the air through your chest and exhaling the air through your chest.

✳ Now bring to mind someone or something that gives you an instant sensation of love or pleasure. Allow those pleasurable feelings to sink deeply into you and spend a few minutes deeply appreciating these people and things that give you pleasure in life.

✳ Once you can feel those sensations of gratitude and love strongly, bring your awareness to the challenging dream. With this attitude of love, breathe into the dream through your heart and allow your mind to come up with three positive reasons why this dream has come up. Don't force your answers, just allow them to arise. Don't judge or edit them, just allow them to appear.

✳ Record your discoveries in your dream journal on the page opposite your original dream if possible.

Children and Nightmares

Nightmares and night terrors are two distinctly different conditions and the latter is such a harrowing experience for parents to witness that I think it's worth talking about it briefly so that you can understand the differences between the two states and manage them.

Recognizing and Dealing with Night Terrors

Although night terrors can appear at any age, they mostly affect children from two to seven or eight years old. They are rare. Although statistics vary from study to study, we're talking between 3 and 15 per cent of children.

Research shows that stress, sleep disruption, trauma and lack of structure can all contribute to the frequency and onset of night terrors. In my experience of healing houses I also believe that sleeping on geopathic stress can be a contributing factor.

Night terrors can be terrifying for parents, as the child genuinely looks terror struck, hence the term. They can have wide staring eyes yet not recognize their parents. Often they let out bloodcurdling screams. Physiologically, they can sweat profusely and have a rapid heartbeat and fast shallow breathing. Sometimes they will sleepwalk or thrash about. In the morning, or if woken up at that moment, they have absolutely no recollection of what's happened and will generally go back to sleep quite happily.

It feels terrifying and powerless for a parent to have to witness this. You love that child and it seems as if they're possessed. It may seem natural to shake them awake, but this shocks the body and the child too deeply. Instead, take a breath, know that your child is absolutely fine, despite current appearances, and just be near them. Gently touch them if you wish, but take care not to restrain them or shake them awake in any way. Soothingly say, 'It's OK. It's all right. We're just here in the bedroom.' Talk gently about normal daily things until the child comes through it. Night terrors are normally of short duration, although they can seem like a lifetime!

Dealing with Children's Nightmares

Children have far more nightmares than adults do because they're processing a lot more unknown and therefore potentially threatening information. The nightmares tend to start at around seven or eight years old – almost at the time when night terrors stop – and to come on in the latter part of the night, during periods of REM sleep. There are no physiological signs. Children do, though, generally have recall of them, which may affect their ability to go back to sleep, as they may be too scared to do so or they may get hooked on the nightmare and it may begin to reoccur.

Here's an example of a typical recurring nightmare from a child brought up in a family where churchgoing and the idea of heaven and hell were part of the waking reality:

In the dream the Devil was chasing me, trying to cut off my head. I remember being utterly terrified by it – it would make me sleepwalk into my parents' bedroom screaming. Once I woke up and was convinced the dream was true because I couldn't see anything and surmised that my head was missing. I had fallen out of bed and my head had landed in the garbage bin beside my bed.

When dealing with children's nightmares we need to actually acknowledge the dream. Most parents automatically say something along the lines of 'Don't worry, it's just a dream. It's not real. Everything's fine. Go back to sleep.' This is, of course, said with love and the best possible intentions, but a more powerful way to deal with the child's nightmare is to acknowledge it with something like 'Wow, that must have been really terrifying. Gosh, what happened then?' You can still talk about it as a dream but actually listen to your child's description of it. This enables them to feel heard and is paradoxically far more reassuring. The child is able to express themselves, able to express their fear, and once a feeling has been felt and acknowledged it can be released.

There's another good reason for attending to your children's dreams. Recurring nightmares in children can be an indication of bullying or trauma of some sort. Remember the unconscious will always feed back what's out of synch through our dreams. A woman on TV recently told me about her daughter who was dreaming that a large truck was coming in through her bedroom window and running her over every night. The truck was massive and felt overwhelming, to the point that the child was too scared to go to sleep despite the fact that she lived on the fourth floor, so no actual truck was likely to crash into her bedroom. It transpired that she had had trouble with a teacher at school recently. Although the situation had been resolved, obviously she still felt powerless and believed that the situation might recur, and the truck that ran her over every night illustrated that.

One of the ways to resolve a child's trauma after a nightmare like this would be to sit down in the morning and talk about the dream. Really listen and pay attention to your child's story. Then ask them to come up with a different ending. Ask them what would be a positive way to end the dream. In the example given above, what magic could happen when that truck hit the window? Maybe the window could be made of rubber and the truck could just bounce off, or fairies could be all lined up at the window protecting the child.

If your child finds working with scary dreams difficult, encourage them to recruit their own dream hero to help them. Perhaps they have a particular toy that could become an heroic figure; for example, Super Ted could come to the rescue. This super being is fearless and knows exactly how to overcome any dream fear. Ask the child what their dream hero would say or do in that scary dream situation. To finish you might like to ask them if there is anything small they'd like to change in their bedroom so that they know the dream has changed now.

The great thing with children's minds and the responsive nature of dreams is that the next time the child has that nightmare they'll have a lucid moment where they remember their dream hero and the nature of the dream will change, especially if you go over it two or three times and really get that positive ending established in their mind. This gives them their power back. They've got something that they can fight back with, something to help them face the fear.

Owning the Nightmare

Engaging with our dreams does require courage – not so much in facing the dreams themselves but in dealing with the deeper understanding of ourselves that results from it. From my experience, not looking at ourselves comes from a desire to see something a set way in order to maintain the illusion of certainty. If we face up to ourselves we have to take responsibility for it. We can no longer blame external factors because we understand they're all part of us. That's a powerful place from which to live. For many of us it's also a terrifying place. It's often easier to pass on the blame. To make excuses for why we're not living the life of our dreams.

Through reflecting on our dreams we'll also become more aware of our life purpose, which may require us to make changes, and change is not a comfortable experience for many of us.

We can face our fears by being gentle, kind and loving to ourselves and by forgiving ourselves. A good question to ask is: 'Would I rather stay as I am or would I rather get to the other side of this?' Always give yourself that choice: 'Do I like where I am or do I want to change? What am I doing this for? What's the purpose of it? What am I looking for? How does this serve me?' If what you're looking for is peace, then ask yourself: 'Is facing this fear going to bring me peace and calm?' If the answer is 'yes', then that's a pretty good return on investment.

So often we get hung up on our feelings. We think we're going to be overwhelmed by them. 'If I get in touch with my anger, I'm going to kill someone.' 'If I start crying, I'll never stop. I'll be crying for months.' Feelings just need to be felt, and once they have been, they just bubble up and disappear. But we get scared of them, so we stick a lid on them and suppress them. A lot of tidal-wave, big blockbuster-type disaster dreams are our unconscious minds having to deal with all the emotional baggage we haven't consciously dealt with. But often just the experience of that in the dream is enough to let it go if we can positively resolve it within the dream itself. Let's look at that now.

We're going to work with the terrifying or scary characters in your dreams. Many shamanic practices deal with dreams in this manner. If someone is suffering with a nightmare, a shaman will take them back into it to heal it.

This next exercise is a way of going back into a dream to get more meaning from it in order to heal it. If you get a dream and it really intrigues you and you've got no idea what it means, then this is also a great way to go in and explore further. Remember you've got all the answers inside you. Everything you need to interpret your dreams is already there, because your psyche made it up. Your psyche knows the answers. So let's see where your psyche takes you.

FACING DREAM SHADOWS

The first stage, as always with dream work, is relaxing, crossing the dreaming bridge into that dreamy meditative state that allows us to access dream messages easily and effortlessly. Use any of the methods mentioned in this book.

Now allow yourself to bring to mind the dream you wish to work with. Allow that dream to become vivid in your imagination. Feel the feelings, hear what was said, see what you saw and notice what you notice.

Recreate the dream fully in your mind and then allow yourself to begin to explore this dream world you have created. Perhaps you'd like to find out what will happen next or maybe there is an aspect of this dream you need to talk to. Why is it there? What is it trying to tell you? What else do you need to understand here? What would be good to know?

Engage in the dream now in whatever way seems perfect for you. No effort is required – just allow your imagination and your psyche to lead you, to guide you to what you notice, what you feel and what you see, always knowing that your inner world will work the perfect way for you. Your unconscious wants to help you. It's its highest motivation; that's why it brings you dreams. So trust it to guide you, to lead you to where you need to be.

Explore the characters and the landscape of this dream. If you get stuck, simply asking, 'And then what could happen?' normally moves you on again.

Do not censor your unconscious – allow it to take you wherever it needs to go. Maybe other characters will appear. That's OK. Allow whatever happens to happen. Don't try to analyse or understand it, just allow it.

When you feel ready, thank your dream and your psyche for their insights and guidance, wiggle your toes and fingers, stretch, open your eyes and come back into your conscious awareness.

Take a few minutes to write down anything that came to you. It may or may not make immediate sense to you. If more symbols and metaphors have appeared, use the exercises to elicit their meaning for you in the same way that you'd work with dream symbols (see *Chapter Five*).

Do you remember the woman who dreamed of a string of cardboard boxes on the sea and felt this was a message about her daughter getting depressed? Here's what she uncovered through this process:

A being came out from one of the boxes. It was a female form in turquoise-green robes and she started talking about freedom and telling me to always be free whatever might be going on in my life, to try to keep that freedom.

Then a second figure came, and I'm not into angels but this was the angel Raphael and he said he was my protection. He hasn't always been nor will he always be, but at this moment he is there.

From another box came a spinning vortex of five coloured lights. I know they were the five elements because on the path that I follow we work a lot with the five elements. The vortex said to me, 'This is the real you.'

And out of the last box came a light misty thing and it said, 'This is your spirit.'

Suddenly this woman has some very real insights into how to deal with her current difficulties, mainly by maintaining her personal freedom, which she obviously feels is threatened in some way, and a real sense of spiritual support. She is concerned about her daughter being ill and Archangel Raphael is specifically the angel of healing.

Here's another example from a woman who was spurned in love in favour of a rival and as a consequence became socially withdrawn:

I went back to the very first dream of my recurring dream sequence. The woman I have been in conflict with was there... I tried to speak to her, as I felt she was part of my problem. She didn't want to know me, though. She just brushed me away, she wouldn't speak to me.

In the original dream, the sky is incredibly black, there are no stars and there's no moon. Today when I revisited the dream there was an angel flying in the sky with a trumpet and then the scene vanished and there was a man sitting in the News 24 studio reading something. I didn't catch what he was reading and I don't understand that.

When you have images that you don't understand, ask in the visualization for clarification. Simply say, 'I don't understand this. Can you tell me what this means?' Work with the process in this way for the best results.

You can also use any of the dream-interpretation processes in this book to work out the messages and symbols you receive. I would interpret the angel with the trumpet as heralding a new dawn after the dark.

There was more from this dreamer, who agreed with that interpretation:

Yes, I felt the darkness was lifting. I was also thinking about the News 24 item. I kept thinking to myself that the last thing I would do normally would be to switch the TV news on, because you tend to get very negative coverage and unpleasant things, and I avoid that. Well, I realize the dream is trying to tell me that I'm avoiding something that I don't want to face up to in my situation. Which makes sense.

Dreams really respond to in-depth research and getting beneath the surface of them.

Use this truth exercise on any dream element that's scary. It works particularly well on stubborn nightmares or recurring dreams that you can't seem to shift.

NIGHTMARE BUSTER

Take something you believe or fear in a dream. For example: 'I am scared of the big bad monster that's chasing me.'

Then ask yourself:

✳ Is it true? Is it always true that I'm scared of the big bad monster?

✳ Is it true in every situation? Even compared with something scarier?'

✳ And when I have that thought about being scared of the big bad monster, then what happens?

✳ ...and then what happens?

✳ Ask this same question six times and when you're finished ask, 'And what do I know now?'

✳ And now what could happen?

Nightmares turn up to make it obvious what we need to be dealing with and what the fear is that we need to face. If we confront it in the ways shown here, then it resolves itself on an emotional level and the fear disappears.

If you can work on this internal cellular level, then your outward life generally provides a solution. Miraculously, you get the email or the phone call or whatever it is you need to sort the situation out. The negative emotion causes tension and once you release it you're no longer creating resistance and so the answers can appear.

Here's a wonderful way to release that emotional resistance and allow the tension to be relieved:

DEALING WITH RECURRING DREAMS AND NIGHTMARES
STEP 1
* Take some paper and fully express the nightmare in whatever shape or form. It could be a drawing, it could be words. Remember the horrid dream feelings as you're doing it. I want you to really tune into those feelings of fear and express them on the page. Write or draw how it is affecting you, how it is making you feel, how it is stressing you out.

* Look at what you've drawn or written, be with it and feel the negative emotions present in your body. Now hold the piece of paper against your body. Tune into the physical feelings inside your body and smile into them. Take a kind, loving attitude to yourself. This is an act of self-compassion, self-love. Gently breathe into and dissolve the feelings, allowing them to melt away inside you. Continue until you feel the emotions simply disappear.

* When the emotions have been released, screw up the piece of paper and throw it in the bin or burn it.

STEP 2
* Write out your nightmare in the present tense, but this time giving it a positive ending, one that *feels* good to you when you tune into it. Really feel the positive emotions in your body.

* When you're done, read it through at least three times. As you read, be aware of what you're feeling physically inside your body. Is it resonating? Can you accept this? Can you allow the good feelings to sink in?

Notice what comes up and again just smile into it. When you get a good feeling, let it sink deeply into you, like a sponge soaking up water. You're not pulling it in, just allowing it to be absorbed into you. Let it sink in at the physical level of the body. It's very subtle, like a sugar cube soaking up tea.

I've taken you through all the steps of this process, but if pushed for time you can just release the negative emotion without doing the positive outcome. Although I think it's ultimately more powerful to do all the parts, releasing the negative emotion will change the dream as it releases layers of tension in your body, allowing your life to ultimately change too.

One older dreamer from my groups had an extraordinarily powerful revelation as a result of doing this process:

My recurring dream theme is that I'm knickerless. I'm often dreaming of two men trying to enter the house. They're either trying to come through the back door or the front door and I'm always closing the doors and trying to close the windows and either I don't have knickers on or I don't have anything on top, but it's never here in the UK, it's in the house in which I grew up abroad.

As I was doing the drawing and feeling the embarrassment inside, it suddenly dawned on me: I've been dreaming these themes for years. Well, I was abused when I was young, from 9 to 14, by the man next door and his son, and that's what it was, that's what I've been dreaming all these years. It was just amazing to realize that and of course the dream is always taking place in the house in which I grew up. As soon as I was drawing it I thought, 'Oh, that's what it is.'

The spell of those dreams has finally been broken for this woman.

We can work with recurring nightmares very successfully in this way. If you fully embrace the process and complete it, your recurring dream will change or disappear because you've resolved it internally, and external changes will then start to take place.

Another woman had this to say of her experience:

For me it was so powerfully simple, it blew me away. I had this awful sickly feeling in my dream that recurred, and changing that into love and joy and peace, how simple is that? And it really worked, that old feeling is completely gone.

And one last example:

My recurring nightmare for years was about doing a theatre show and getting on the wrong bus or train and ending up going in the wrong direction and not knowing how to get back to where I started and knowing that there were people waiting for me there and that I was going to be late for rehearsal and late for the show and in fact was probably never going to be able to find my way back, and I was thinking, 'What am I doing here?'

When I held that against myself I went into a panic. I had a real fluttery and panicky feeling about being lost. Then, when I did the part about how to resolve the dream, it said I must now believe in my ability to move forward in the direction I know is right for me and it's my journey and I'm not responsible for other people, as they have their own journey. Now I will be on the right mode of transport to a destination that is perfect for me and I'll enjoy the journey and trust in it.

Another way to resolve negative dream emotions is to do the following:

WRITING NEW DREAMS

✳ Take two sheets of paper. On the first sheet write out your nightmare in the first person, present tense. If you've got limited time just work with the really terrifying bit, the finale or climax. Really feel the emotions associated with it as you write it out. It won't feel good, yet the more you feel it, the more you will release it. Also describe what you don't want to happen in this dream, i.e. the thing that was probably about to happen when you woke yourself up!

✳ Now take the second piece of paper. On this write how you'd like to feel instead. How would you like that dream to work out in a positive fashion? Remember you're the hero at the centre of your dreams, they're yours to choose.

✳ When you've finished, read over what you've written and really feel the positive emotions this new dream evokes. Own it, inside.

✳ Finally burn the first piece of paper and place the second under your pillow and sleep on it for a week. The dream will change.

This exercise can also be used with any recurring dream theme or element.

Now here's a way to turn a scary dream round entirely:

CHANGING YOUR SCARY DREAM INTO A PLEASANT DREAM

✳ Think of the thing you most love to do or that's most important to you. Bring this vividly to mind now.

✳ Notice the details of the picture this creates in your mind:

Are you looking through your own eyes or are you outside yourself watching yourself in the picture?

Is the picture in black and white or colour?

Are the images sharp or blurry?

Is it like watching a movie or seeing a photograph?

Is the scene moving quickly or slowly?

Does the picture seem close to you or far away?

Are the sounds and voices you can hear loud or quiet?

Is there a positive emotion that you can feel in your physical body that's associated with this image?

Are there any other particular attributes of this positive scene?

∗ You may like to jot down all these attributes of your favourite scene as a reminder and to make the exercise quicker next time round.

∗ Now bring to mind the picture of your scary dream and notice how it differs from the above. For example, it might be in black and white whilst your pleasurable images are in colour.

∗ Each time you encounter a difference, change your nightmare element to match that aspect of your pleasurable memory. For example, change your nightmare image from black and white into colour. Each time you change an attribute, spend a short while making sure you can easily see the new positive attribute associated with the old scary image.

∗ Continue to do this until you can see the nightmare in the same way that you can see the pleasurable experience. Notice that the negative emotions associated with the nightmare have disappeared now.

TOP TIPS FOR RESOLVING NIGHTMARES

* Face your fears. Ask questions. For example, if you're being chased, ask: 'What am I running from in my life?' If trapped, ask: 'What aspect of my life makes me feel trapped?'

* Write a new ending. If you have a recurring nightmare, write it out and create a new positive ending.

* Tell somebody the nightmare a minimum of three times.

* Visualize going back into it whilst awake and use your imagination to give it a happy ending.

* Write out the dream from the perspective of the 'bad' character(s). This helps to uncover the fear you're running from.

Michael Brandon, the American actor famous for his leading roles in the TV series *Dempsey & Makepeace* and *Jerry Springer, the Opera*, helped other actors overcome stage fright by using a nightmare-resolution technique. In acting workshops, he would get actors to play out the following nightmare to resolve their fear:

Every night a monster is chasing me down a dark alley. Each night it gets closer. I can feel its tentacled fingers grabbing my shoulder. I am running as fast as I can, but I can feel its hot fetid breath on my neck and hear its awful hissing growl in my ears.

Each night the dream continues until one night I come to the end of the alley. It's bricked up. There's nowhere to run. It's a dead end.

I turn and face the monster. It's more horrific than I could ever have imagined. It's right in front of me. It's got me and there is no escape.

I scream, 'What do you want from me?'

The monster stops and says, 'I don't know. It's your dream, man.'

The message of the dream: face your fear and it will dissolve.

By this stage you should be feeling great, having released all those negative nightmare emotions, and you have tonnes of great new skills for dealing with any future nightmares and recurring dreams. So now it's time for the grand dreaming finale, how to use your dreams to access your genius potential, that latent talent within waiting to be unleashed.

CHAPTER ELEVEN

Unlock your Inner Einstein

The Magic of Creative Dreaming

'To live a creative life, we must lose our fear of being wrong.'
Joseph Chilton Pearce

Imagination is our greatest gift – the gift of our dreaming mind both whilst asleep and whilst awake. Our greatest limitation in creating new learning is simply a lack of imagination. With imagination, we can fill in the empty spaces in our minds with endless new ideas, new discoveries and understandings, and wonderful new insights will emerge. All we have to do is dream.

Although this chapter is vital in terms of your creative potential, I've saved it until last for a reason. By now you'll have used the exercises in this book to work through some of your dreams. As a result, you'll have developed trust in the extraordinary capability and intelligence of your dreaming mind. You need that to get the most out of your creative dreaming. If you dream the perfect solution to your problem but it turns up as a nonsense dream, you may be tempted to ignore it. But now you know that even a nonsense dream will unlock hidden gems, you'll decipher it with pleasure in anticipation of the insights that will be revealed.

Research has proven that when we are deprived of sleep it's our creativity that disappears first, along with our ability to focus and concentrate. When we're finally allowed to catch up on our sleep we'll spend longer in REM sleep than normal, catching up on our creative processes.

During REM sleep, as we now know, the body shuts down the logical, rational part of the brain and floods our system with its most creative chemicals. We can utilize this amazing and entirely natural resource to our advantage. Why not engage with this most potent part of yourself? This is where the true power of your dreaming mind begins to be unlocked. If you can capture that creative input, you can then use your conscious logical mind to put those snippets of genius into action.

Lenny Henry, in a 'A Life in the Day' interview for the *Sunday Times* on 6 September 2009, talked about writing a screenplay and using the creative forces of his dreamtime: 'There are writing days when I get up at six and come down and just start writing. My brain is still bubbling, still in a weird dream state. That's when the best ideas come.'

Here's another true story, from the film director Nigel Spence, that perfectly illustrates the power of our dreaming intelligence:

My wife showed me the local newspaper: 'Look, darling, a boy's been murdered in the next village. There's a £5,000 reward for information leading to the arrest of the murderer. We could do with that. Why don't you meditate, dream or whatever you do and find the murderer?'

That night before I fell asleep I asked the powers that be – that higher intelligence – that if they wanted to use me as an agent for good, they could tell me who the murderer was.

I dreamed I walked into a farmyard. There was a yellow forklift truck parked on the right-hand side of the yard and

*black and white Friesen cows in front of me. Overhead was
a corrugated tin roof and straw lay on the ground of the
cattle pens. I heard two voices talking to each other. A man
drove the yellow forklift truck across the yard in front of me,
shouting at a farm worker feeding the cattle.*

*In the far corner of the cattle enclosure was a small pen
to protect a newborn calf. In the pen was the dead body of a
boy. The forklift driver and the farm worker were burying him
under straw and mud. I awoke.*

*That day a farmer I'd met at a party three years before
asked for professional advice on his computer system, which I
agreed to supply.*

*The next day I walked into his farmyard for the first time.
There was a yellow forklift truck parked on the right-hand
side of the yard and black and white Friesen cows in front of
me. It was the precise farmyard that I had dreamed of.*

*A voice shouted at me, 'Oi, you, move your bloody car!' I
recognized that voice. It was the voice I'd heard in my dream
– that of the farm worker who had been helping the forklift
truck driver. I asked who the man shouting at me was and was
told it was the next-door farmer.*

*Later I told the police about the farmyard. Within a year
(the wheels of justice and court hearings work slowly), the
forklift driver was convicted and imprisoned for the murder of
the boy.*

One mystery of the dreaming mind is that we can set an
intention for our dream, but we can never predict what we'll
dream. However, our dreaming mind is far more intelligent
than our conscious mind and it will give us what we need to
know. So we can ask for an answer, ask for insight, ask for
clarity, ask for guidance. We can even ask for understanding
about a dream that we had the previous night.

We tend to think of creativity as the domain of the artist,
the musician, the novelist, the poet, the painter. Yet we're all

creative to a lesser or greater degree. The essence of creativity is simply the ability to find a solution to a problem. We all possess this innate talent and it is profoundly the domain of our dreaming minds. During the dream phase of sleep we're solution-seeking missiles on a quest for the truth. We can all access this power. From the Buddha to the Bible we've heard 'The answers lie within' and 'As a man thinketh, so he becomes' and our dreams hold the key.

To be truly creative, we have to be curious. When we engage with our curiosity, we step away from perceiving things as we always have and allow ourselves to get new perspectives on familiar terrain. Think how many times Edison must have done that in his epic attempts to create the light bulb. As he said himself, 'If I find 10,000 ways something won't work, I haven't failed. I am not discouraged, because every wrong attempt discarded is another step forward.' He was able to continually shift his perspective on the light bulb and see a new path, a new way of doing things, until he finally succeeded.

Sleep on It

A friend of mine, Sven Lorenz, has the ability to run global multi-disciplinary businesses. His output is extraordinarily prolific and I've often wondered over the years how he manages to keep up with it all. Recently I've found he uses his dreams. He claims not to consciously remember them. However, he puts them to work just the same by always skim-reading material he needs to work on before going to sleep and musing on it as he falls asleep. When he wakes, he declares the answers are just there.

I've used a similar process myself before workshops or important presentations or seminars, and I take it a step further and quite literally do sleep on it by putting the relevant materials under my pillow the night before. The results are always remarkable and pertinent. For me, this is nothing more than giving myself absolutely the best opportunity to do the best job I can at any given moment. Why wouldn't we use all the tools we have at our disposal? There are no guarantees of success in life. But I do believe in giving myself permission to go for something 100 per cent, and using my dreams is part of that process.

Nothing man-made would exist on the planet without imagination and dreams. Creative dreaming is hugely powerful and transformative. One of my favourite dream stories concerns Elias Howe, who invented the sewing machine. He was on the verge of bankruptcy because of this sewing machine. He'd been trying every method and couldn't get it to work and he couldn't understand why. Then he dreamed of being surrounded by a Zulu tribe, all with spears ready to attack him. He noticed in the dream that the spears had holes in the pointed tips facing him. When he woke up, he got the solution to his problem by putting the hole in the other end of the needle.

Of course you've got to be able to understand how to make the leap from Zulus with spears to your sewing machine. Which is where all the dream-translation techniques you've learned really come into their own.

Sometimes our creative dreams are more succinct, as illustrated by this inspirational dream from the much-loved actress, singer and now author Martine McCutcheon:

I had been thinking of doing a TV show. I remember I wanted it to be a mixture of a Working Title film and the Ally McBeal surreal moments. I wanted bizarre moments to happen in some heightened sense of reality because I felt I wanted to capture the romance, the bit of magic adults are still allowed to have. It was really on my mind to do something, to create something for myself, but I didn't know at that point what it was going to be.

Then I had a dream in which I was running upstairs in the most beautiful high heels, fashion out of the 1930s or 1940s. I was wearing a peachy chiffon dress and a vintage kind of fur throw. I was running up the stairs in the rain and got into a taxi. The driver was talking to me but I was preoccupied. I knew I was going somewhere important because I felt really excited.

I went into a restaurant which looked like the Wolseley in London. Everything colour-wise was heightened, anything that would normally shine was sparkling – it was all very vivid. I felt an excitement in the air. I could see all my friends – they were all giving me hugs and kisses. It was some kind of celebration, only I didn't know what the celebration was.

Then I saw the most gorgeous man staring at me from over at the bar. He had a friend with him who was dressed in a raincoat and he was packing his briefcase away as they were talking. But he wasn't really listening to the guy at all, he just kept looking at me, looking at me, looking at me, to the point that it took my breath away. I felt as though I couldn't sit down. I could feel his eyes burning through me, so I made my excuses with my friends and went down into the bathroom, which was all marble and black with ornate lamps. I remembered I had perfume, Chanel perfume, with me. It's the perfume I had when I was filming in Austria and it brought back the excitement of the movie. I sprayed the perfume over myself and started doing my make-up in anticipation of seeing the man again. I was excited by the thought of seeing him.

On my way back to the table he talked to me. My breath was completely taken away by his smell and how close he wanted to get to me. The next thing I remember I was sitting at a table and looked up and he'd gone. There was no trace of him. It felt as though it was too good to be true and it turned out it was – it was a dream!

At the time I thought this was something that was going to happen in my love life. It turned out to be an idea for a TV show and Chapter One of my bestselling book The Mistress.

Dream School

Because creativity is in reality the ability to solve something, learning is a highly developed function of the dreaming mind. Recent scientific research has illustrated how dreaming about an activity can dramatically improve our performance in waking life. New studies have shown that if you play complex games like Dungeons and Dragons before going to sleep and then actually dream of that activity, you can get better results in the games the following morning. Similarly, watching a video of a perfect ski performance just before you go to bed will enable you, especially if you dream about it, to improve your performance on the slopes the next day. The golfer Jack Nicklaus once had an issue with his golf swing. In a dream he saw himself correcting the swing and doing it perfectly. When he tested out the dream method the next day, it solved the problem. My husband, a professional musician and composer, often dreams of writing music in his sleep, which constantly inspires his creative output during the day.

One of the most remarkable examples of this type of dream learning came from a friend of mine. Here's her story:

My earliest recall of dreams that made a difference was when I was 16. I was an apprentice hairdresser and really struggling with nerves and lack of confidence. My employers could see my potential and admired my work ethic but were concerned that my anxieties were holding me back with practicalities such as putting hair in rollers and perm curlers, as I would physically tremble so much that I couldn't get them to stay in the hair! Then I had a succession of dreams over three nights where I could see myself standing behind a client, no one I knew, confidently putting rollers and curlers in their hair over and over and over again. The dreams were so vivid that they felt physical. Each night I would improve and become faster, more adept and work successfully on the task with increased confidence.

After this series of dreams I did turn into the girl in the dreams and everyone was completely baffled as to how I had managed to turn things around.

After this my hairdressing career went from strength to strength. I was sent to Vidal Sassoon Academy for training and was made manageress at the age of 18.

To students everywhere it seems there's a lot to be said for having an early night before an exam rather than staying up all night cramming.

Power Dream Naps

Successful people who sleep less than normal but are highly creative and productive often rely on power naps to refresh themselves mentally. They may only sleep four hours a night but take regular power naps during the day, perhaps a 20-minute nap twice a day. This can be a phenomenally creative thing to do, especially, if you use this four-step dreaming process in conjunction with your nap:

1. Tune into what you need to know.
2. Scan any documents or books you have in relation to the issue. Alternatively, just mull it over in your mind.
3. Relax into your power nap, deciding that you will wake with the perfect solution to your problem.
4. Limit the power nap to 20–25 minutes. If you go beyond this it tends to be less effective because you transit into deep sleep and will wake up feeling groggy. Twenty minutes is the optimum time for a restorative power nap. It's interesting to note it's the same length of time many teachers recommend for meditation, which, of course, is an excellent alternative to the power nap.

Here's a great power nap example from Georgie Fame, the legendary singer, keyboard player and songwriter:

I did a lot of collaborating with the late Steve Grey, a wonderful composer and arranger. He'd done a library album of big-band music and had written a romantic, tender melody. Its original title was 'Will Carling', who, at the time, was captain of the England rugby team. The publishers of the album didn't like that title, so they made him call it 'Angel Dust', but he wanted it to be 'Will Carling'. He sent me the recording and asked if I could write some lyrics for it. I listened to it and it was quite beautiful. The first obstacle was, well, if it's 'Will Carling', how do you write something romantic and tender? But Steve told me he had called it 'Will Carling' because it reminded him of the famous song 'Lil' Darlin'', composed by Neil Hefti for the Count Basie Orchestra, so at least I had something to go on.

I still didn't know where to start with it, though. It was a weekend, so I had lunch and went into the TV room. There was an international rugby game on, England were playing somebody and Will Carling was the captain. I started to watch the game and fell asleep. I had a romantic dream, a domestic dream about my wife and myself and our environment. I woke up as Will Carling was scoring a try, I think it was his second try, and I thought, 'Bloody hell, what's going on here?' and I went back to sleep and then when I woke up I realized what had happened and I wrote this whole lyric there and then:

A beautiful morning with skies of blue.

Out under the awning next to you.

The winter wind and snow have gone and our love blossoms in the sun.

What joy I feel aglow inside,

As evening descends on a rosy hue,

A candlelit dinner's laid for two.

I suddenly awake and wipe my sleepy eye

As Will Carling scores another try.

Then all I had to do was resolve it, using a bit of artistic licence, and I had gone back to sleep, so the last bit is:

When slumber reclaims me again you are near,
And promise no more to disappear.
I hold you in my arms and then I realize
it's me not Will Carling scoring tries.

Use this next technique for increasing your access to the hypnogogic state, where we can access the power of our hypnotic mind. This is not my invention – both Salvador Dali and Sir Isaac Newton used it regularly, although in slightly different ways, and my version is closer to Newton's, as in my experience it works better. I encourage you to experiment with the idea, though, and find the way that best works for you. It takes the power of the catnap to a completely new level.

CREATIVE CATNAPS

This is easiest if practised whilst sleeping in a chair or on the sofa, i.e. those places we tend to choose for our daytime naps.

Either read through the material pertaining to your problem or bring it to mind in the normal way that you would do for a power nap. The difference is, in one of your upturned palms you're going to place a marble, or something equivalent. In the past I have used a battery, a heavy pen and a teaspoon. However, a marble is an excellent choice as it fits neatly in your curled palm without you having to exert any effort to hold on to it. This is key to a successful hypnogogic experience.

Your awareness of the object should be similar to a meditation practice, i.e. the relationship between the object and the subject should be as two feathers touching. More effort than this creates tension in the mind and will exhaust rather than refresh you. You need to get into that space where you trust your unconscious mind to do its own thing and deliver information that is currently just outside your parameters of awareness. It's the coach shouting at you from the touchlines, but you're stuck in midfield and can only hear lost whispers echoing in the breeze.

When you relax deeply enough, you can let go into the space where you trust your unconscious mind. And the beauty of holding the marble is that when you reach the optimum point of relaxation, it will fall from your hand, preferably onto something like a wooden floor or a tin tray, something that will make enough noise to awake you from your slumber.

Immediately record any of the thoughts, mind pictures or ideas that are with you in that moment.

You'll be astonished at the solutions to problems you receive and the inspiration you get from indulging regularly in this practice. It is far superior to using some kind of alarm to wake you after 20 minutes, as it corresponds perfectly to your body's unique ability to go into the hypnogogic phase, which of course can vary enormously from person to person. To begin with, as you are unused to the method you may find you hold too much tension in the hand holding the marble and fail to allow yourself to ever reach the critical state. The trick is to just keep relaxing and letting go of tension in your body whilst keeping the problem in your mind's eye, not becoming fixated on it in a rigid way.

Often the information you receive is precise and immediate, whilst at other times it's more obscure or symbolic and it takes longer for the penny to drop. The more impatient amongst you can apply any of the dream-interpretation techniques given in this book to the information you receive in these hypnogogic dream states. That will allow you to unravel meaning from nonsense!

Creative Daydreaming

I'm a master daydreamer and value the benefits it brings to my life. Even amidst the busiest of days with deadlines looming I will take a few precious minutes here and there just to stop and stare. My husband often asks, 'Where were you just then?' as he can clearly see I'm not present in the room, despite the fact that my eyes are open. In those moments distractions, sound and activity have disappeared from my awareness. I just am. It is akin to being everywhere and nowhere all at once. When I return, my energy is immediately renewed and I can often return to the issue I was working on – a difficult email, a report, a workshop, a chapter – and find it flows easily again. The problems are solved and I know exactly what to say. I'm sure many of you do exactly the same thing, it's just that you've never thought much about it before. This is a valid creative process, though, that we can actively engage in and reap benefits from in many areas. It is particularly useful if you are dealing with something tricky that you're not sure about or you've got a creative block.

The technique is akin to a power nap but simpler and quicker:

DREAM GAZING

Simply pause where you're working and, taking your problem with you, gaze into space.

Gradually let the problem drift away from your mind as you continue to gaze softly into space.

It helps to have a distant view to stare at. Your awareness needs to be able to travel and that's easier if the mind can get lost in the view. If this isn't possible, take your awareness through whatever is in your path. For example, if you are confronted by a wall, think what's beyond the wall and drift off into that realm. Or you can close your eyes and visualize a distant, peaceful place. Travel to that place, make yourself at home, feel the calm and review your problem from there for a few minutes.

Creative-solution Dreams

Thinking outside the box is greatly enhanced by the chemicals that are released during the dream cycle. Solution dreams tap into that potent resource. I'm going to discuss a couple of ways you can access this in this section. They follow a similar format.

One of the big issues with dreams is they lack a specific context. We get information that could relate to anything in life. This makes it more challenging to elicit truth from dreams, as we can allow our natural biases to sway us in how we interpret them. We eliminate this problem by giving a dream a specific issue to work with. That is, we set the dream up, we give the answer a context. Otherwise, we can get the answer to a question we didn't know we'd asked.

Here's how legendary American pianist, composer and arranger Roger Kellaway used this process:

My 'Visions of America' symphonic project, with simultaneous projected photos, premiered last 25 January in Philly as a 'Photo-Symphony' with the Philly Pops, Peter Nero conducting. I was the jazz soloist, Patti Austin the vocalist.

Since it is now going to be performed by the Philadelphia Symphony Orchestra and not the Pops, I spent nine hours in a dream sifting through all that I had composed so far for the first draft première. All of the composition and orchestration transformed to a higher and fuller musical level. I asked, clearly, to link with the Cosmos during this process so that those in need could be healed by the transformative results.

I believe that I'm now in a higher place creatively because of this dream. Time will tell.

Invoking dream solutions is based on ancient dream incubation practices, modern versions created by psychologists and our problem-solving equation from Chapter Four: 'The problem plus resources equals a solution.' Within the context of creative dreaming the conscious mind recognizes the problem and utilizes the vast resources of the dreaming mind to conjure up potential answers. Once you're practised in the art of creative dreaming, you can speed up the process, but to start with give yourself a good 20 to 30 minutes to prepare your dreaming attention.

To ensure optimum success there are a few points to be aware of. First, our old friend *intention*. Set the intention that you will have a dream that you will clearly remember that will directly answer your problem. Without that initial desire, forget it, you're not going to get a decent dream, because you need desire in order to dream.

Next, you need to pick an issue that is truly important to you, someone or something you feel strongly enough about to ensure you're engaged at an emotional level, as our unconscious rules the emotions.

You also need to be prepared to act on the answer you get. For example, if you're asking about a relationship but know in your heart that if the dream advice were to walk out on that person, you'd ignore it, then ask a different question. Your psyche doesn't respond to you messing around with it on that level. It's about being truthful. It's no good lying to ourselves – it doesn't help anyone, least of all ourselves. I appreciate it's a brave way to live. It's also a fantastic way to live, an inspiring and life-changing way, but it does take courage.

So begin gently by asking about something that you feel it's possible to solve. You can go deeper later, when you've built trust in the power of your dream solutions.

CREATING DREAM SOLUTIONS

✳ Set an intention for a clear dream answer. Dreams respond to desire.

✳ Choose an issue that's truly important to you and be ready to act on the answer you seek.

✳ Ask a question you feel it is possible to get an answer to.

✳ Consciously work on the problem for a few minutes. Either in your mind or mind map the issue on paper. Maybe illustrate it with pictures.

How have you tried to solve this problem?

What does this issue mean to you?

For what purpose do you need to solve the problem?

What will happen as a result of solving this?

What will happen if you don't solve it?

✳ Complete this process by encapsulating the issue in a single question. Be careful with this. Your dream will answer exactly what you ask, so ensure your request is as clear and unambiguous as possible. Write down the final question in your dream journal and date it. You may like to sleep with it under your pillow!

✳ Go to sleep with minimal distractions and mull over the situation in question. Feel what it would be like to get the perfect answer and believe that you will.

✳ Repeat the dream question over and over in your mind as you drift off to sleep.

＊ If you wake during the night, *write down* any dreams, dream fragments, thoughts or feelings. Go back to sleep repeating the dream question.

＊ In the morning, lie still, collect your dream thoughts, then record everything you received.

＊ Use previous exercises to interpret any dream symbols, characters, archetypes, etc. that you don't understand.

＊ Trust the information you receive.

This is the basic process. You can use it on anything you want an answer to, anything from 'What's the best way for me to lose weight?' to 'What do I need to know to progress my business?' and pretty much anything in between. In my experience, I find the solution appears over two to three nights of dreaming, with each dream adding to the one before it. You'll get fantastic results, it's a really fun process to start using and as an added bonus it automatically improves your dream recall. Whenever I use this process I always get a dream I remember, whereas if I just go to sleep I sometimes remember my dreams and sometimes not. It's because we're using our conscious mind to specifically engage with our unconscious, and our unconscious is under the direction of the conscious, so it has to respond.

Know your unconscious responds with your absolute best interests at heart; it never gives you the wrong answer. If you get what seems to be the wrong answer, it's because you didn't ask the right question or you don't yet understand the answer you've received. Remember you can always go back and ask for clarification. You can also use one of the techniques we have used here, like going back into it through meditation, to explore further.

There's also another process where we can be more fluid with our dreaming mind if we're not concerned with gathering evidential information that we need to take action on. If we just want to work with our dream to resolve something without needing to consciously understand it, we can program our dreaming mind with multiple questions and allow the Dream Whisperer to do its work in its own way. I would recommend doing this process as a weekend dream retreat or even a week retreat process.

DREAM MULTIPLIER

✱ Follow the normal dream preparation rules in terms of relaxing the mind for sleep.

✱ Write down in your dream journal your multiple intentions for this process. For example, 'I want to know how to work with my creativity and sort out my relationship with my partner and move house and deal with my job and look after my children properly and find all the money that I want in order to do that.' Your list can be virtually endless.

✱ Just read this intention out loud to yourself before going to sleep each night and allow the dreaming mind to work on the issues for you.

With this process, you don't actively analyse anything, just sleep through the process and see what happens. You've set the intention and handed over the instructions to your unconscious mind, which will obediently set to work for you as it is programmed to do. Of course, if there are underlying beliefs blocking your intentions that your unconscious cannot solve, it will let you know through a nightmare or recurring dream, which you can then deal with as or if it occurs.

The Akashic Records

We're going to enjoy one last creative process that will allow you to access whatever it is you need to know. This is a journey which you may like to record on tape and play back to yourself.

The Akashic Records are a mythological text. Imagine a Domesday Book of the entire universe where everything that ever was and will be is recorded. These records are the ultimate source of all information, the origin of all knowledge. We can journey to find them.

We can access the Akashic Records because they're a visionary tool for utilizing the quantum field. The Akashic Records and the quantum field could in fact be seen as one and the same, the basic state from which all phenomena arise. The Akashic Records are simply a more user-friendly version for our imaginations to grasp than plain old quantum consciousness. It's a more visual version of the data stream but it's still the data stream. So we can use it to source the origin of events, see future outcomes and find information.

AN AKASHIC JOURNEY

Close your eyes, relax, breathe, meditate... Give yourself permission to journey ... and set your intention. What is it you seek?

Find yourself in a clear desert landscape. You can see for miles around in every direction. You begin to walk ... and continue to walk ... and walk until you come upon a vast clear crystal pyramid that towers above you...

You walk up to the entrance, up the crystal steps and through the glittering entrance into the antechamber. On a golden table in the centre of the pyramid lies a large ornate book.

Walk over and see that it's entitled 'The Akashic Records'.

Refocus for a moment on your original intention for this journey ... then open the book...

Immediately the pages start to flip forward and back. You can clearly see the lands and places and events in every page...

The book pauses at a certain page. Note the date at the top of the page and allow the scene in front of you to unfold in whatever way it chooses... Feel what you feel, hear what you hear, see what you see and notice what you notice...

When you feel ready, close the book ... and retrace your steps back through the glittering entrance and down the crystal steps to the desert and walk ... and walk back into now.

Wiggle your toes and fingers and stretch. Have a quick shake and write down any insights, learning and discoveries in your journal.

I often get asked how to make practical use of the information received on a guided journey or in a dream. There's a very simple answer: it's called *Take Action*! Dream information is only meaningful if you bother to act on the information that you get.

This is beautifully illustrated by this dream from Clarke Peters, the American actor, singer, writer and director best known for his role as Detective Lester Freamon on HBO drama *The Wire*:

In 1986 I started studying yoga with the Brahma Kumaris. After about a year, I was going to meet the heads of the organization. I think part of the dream was due to the anticipation of having this meeting with them.

In my dream three or four of them showed up and one of them, I think it was Dadi Janki, gave me five diamonds. The first thing I said was 'Wow!' because I didn't realize that diamonds had weight. I still don't know whether they do or not, but a cut diamond and a cut piece of glass the same size are not going to feel the same in your hand. I remember being in my dream, feeling these five diamonds and thinking, 'This is great,' and 'What am I going to do with this?'

Nine months later the musical I'd been creating, Five Guys Named Moe, *based on the greatest hits of Louis Jordan, came out and ran for five years. I realized that dream had resonated with me all that time and influenced my actions.*

Only by connecting with the dreaming spirit inside our hearts can we evolve towards truth, love, freedom and joy. As Jung said, 'Who looks outside dreams, who looks inside awakens.' When we develop the compassion for ourselves that allows us to let our hearts dream freely by engaging with our internal dreams, the external dream will just as surely change.

You're on the journey. The Dream Whisperer has awoken inside you and you're beginning to dream your dreams awake. May you continue to engage with them and realize the extraordinary potential for creative genius that lies within.

Afterword

'The unexamined life is not worth living.'
Socrates

Congratulations for having come this far. Now your personal dream journey begins in earnest. I hope the exercises you have worked through have inspired you to realize that dreams are not quite the mystery they first appeared to be. I encourage you to continue, as the personal rewards of paying attention to your dreaming are an unlimited resource of creativity, ideas, solutions, self-knowledge and healing.

We're all unique and we all process information differently, which is why a wide variety of different dream techniques has been included here. Please choose the ones that have worked best for you and continue to use those. Perhaps later you will experiment with other journeys and exercises within the book to widen your dream repertoire. Please persevere, as the more you work with dreams, the easier it becomes to unlock their secrets. Already you will have seen the truth of this in how the quality of your dream recall has improved by reading this book and becoming more aware of your dreaming mind.

When we learn any new skill, from learning to walk to driving a car to speaking another language, at the beginning it's tough and mistakes are made. Nevertheless, gradually our skill improves and eventually we no longer have to think about how to walk or drive the car or speak the language; we can do it effortlessly. It has become part of us. The same is true for your dreams, except it is far simpler, as dreams are already part of you and, contrary to appearances, they want to be understood! And the more you work with these dream exercises, the more quickly and easily the revelations and insights will come. Soon you'll hardly need the exercises, as you'll be attuned to your own personal dream language and the meanings of your night-time movies will be easily apparent to you. Yet even as you become your own dream expert, this book will remain an excellent source of dream inspiration. If you're ever stuck with a dream, just close your eyes and open a page at random and see what is revealed there and how it relates to the dream you're working on.

Never worry about anything dream related. Worry creates tension, which limits our ability to hear the dreaming messages of our unconscious and blocks our healing potential. If you miss a dream there's always another night, another dream, another chance to begin again. If the message is important it will become a recurring dream theme until you do have time to stop and address the issue. That's the beauty of our unconscious – it remembers everything and constantly reports what is and what isn't working to our conscious mind through our dreams. All we have to do is pay attention and learn the language of these nightly reports. As we've discovered, sometimes the Me, Inc. workforce doesn't have to bring our attention to an unresolved issue but can process the information for us and we can read the dream report later or choose to ignore it, knowing that if there's an issue that needs our attention a powerful dream will occur.

Dreams will always highlight our dark side, helpfully pointing out the disowned aspects of ourselves that cause us pain in our waking reality. So make friends with your dreams, for they, above all else, will tell you exactly how things are. Unlike some of our real friends, dreams don't lie to us to save face or cover up the truth to protect our feelings. If you want to know the truth and reclaim your power and wholeness, listen carefully to the messages of your Dream Whisperer.

Already you will have discovered some of your secrets and realized that nothing in your dreams is wasted or nonsensical. Dreams provide you with the most powerful tool of personal therapy and transformation. They can also provide you with creative solutions to all your problems. Working with dreams is a process of awakening to what you already know, understanding how extraordinary and powerful you truly are and thus allowing yourself to create more of who you really are in the world. It is a journey, a process of unfolding, an exciting adventure to be treasured and honoured, to play with and enjoy.

The golden key for unlocking this lifetime adventure is to record your dreams. As your personal dream journal grows, so will your self-discovery, self-knowledge and self-worth. Take what you need from this book when you need it and trust your dreaming mind to lead you always towards your inner truth, your authentic self.

You now have the knowledge to unlock the power of your dreams. I wish you every success and, of course, the very sweetest of dreams.

Appendix

Dream Symbols – Some Interpretations

Major Arcana Archetype	Key Attributes
The Fool (The divine child/ innocent/hero/adventurer archetype):	*Positive:* Decisions, independence, initiative, innocence, a leap of faith, trust, fearlessness, new beginnings, new perspectives, spontaneity, optimism, a carefree outlook.
	Shadow: Irresponsibility. An unrealistic dreamer playing the fool. Fear of change, playing with fire, inexperience.
Numerology:	0
Astrology:	Uranus
The Magician (The trickster/creator/ alchemist/artist archetype):	*Positive:* Intention, focus, will power, energy, synthesis, manifestation, education, new skills, discipline, problem solving, confidence.
	Shadow: Not using talents, misuse of power, lack of skills, loss of power, trickery, weakness, low self-worth.
Numerology:	1
Astrology:	Mercury
The High Priestess (The goddess/virgin/ counsellor/fairy godmother archetype):	*Positive:* Connection with the inner world, guidance, hunches, dreams, the occult, mysteries, truth, self-trust, secrets, psychological insight, celibacy.
	Shadow: Judgement, over-analysis, mistrust of inner voice, ignoring messages, procrastination, manipulation, hysteria, superficiality.
Numerology:	2
Astrology:	Moon
The Empress (The mother/ grandmother/anima archetype):	*Positive:* Love, affection, networking, celebration, abundance, fertility, living the good life, feminine sexuality, motherhood.
	Shadow: Greed, complacency, hard-heartedness, infertility, chaos, gossip, stagnation, loss of child(ren), failure to thrive.
Numerology:	3
Astrology:	Venus

Major Arcana Archetype	Key Attributes
The Emperor (The father/ grandfather/animus archetype):	*Positive:* Order, control, power, structure, foundation, status, a conservative outlook, stability, ambition, law and order, wisdom. *Shadow:* Stagnation, inflexibility, stubbornness, a miserly attitude, all work and no play, rigidity, a wimpish approach, the abuse of power, the Peter Pan syndrome, tyranny.
Numerology:	4
Astrology:	Aries
The Hierophant (The god/ priest/teacher/wise man/ persona archetype):	*Positive:* Ethical values, moral wisdom, socialization, tradition, orthodoxy, convention, spiritual growth, conformity, learning, culture. *Shadow:* Fundamentalism, dishonesty, breaking rules, social isolation, stubbornness, close-mindedness, propaganda.
Numerology:	5
Astrology:	Taurus
The Lovers (The relationship/soul mate/ marriage/Don Juan archetype):	*Positive:* Conscious decisions, choice, romance, marriage, sharing, relationships, a turning point, a crossroads, trust, duality, union, health. *Shadow:* Indecision, divorce, bad relationships, disharmony, temptation, fear of commitment, hedonism, arguments, separation.
Numerology:	6
Astrology:	Gemini
The Chariot (The doer/ integrator/messenger archetype):	*Positive:* Choices, travel, initiation, confrontation, rites of passage, leaving home, a clear purpose, conquest, mastery, single-mindedness. *Shadow:* Imbalance, reckless action, temptation, the inability to cut ties, failure, indulgence, laziness, being tied to the apron strings, feeling overwhelmed.
Numerology:	7
Astrology:	Cancer
Strength (The courage/ warrior archetype):	*Positive:* Internal and external strength, digging deep, fortitude, endurance, stamina, overcoming fears, power, confidence, heroism. *Shadow:* Weakness, cowardice, being bullied, dependency, depression, timidity, temper tantrums, being confrontational, being argumentative.
Numerology:	8
Astrology:	Leo

Major Arcana Archetype	Key Attributes
The Hermit (The loner/ wise man/inner teacher archetype):	*Positive:* Quietness, reflection, solitude, going within, self-discovery, self-knowledge, meditation, peace, patience, discretion, wisdom, contemplation.
	Shadow: Isolation, loneliness, self-deception, withdrawal, self-delusion, exile, bereavement, rashness, escapism, false pride, egotism.
Numerology:	9
Astrology:	Virgo
The Wheel of Fortune (The luck/gambler archetype):	*Positive:* Life's ups and downs, changes, karma, lessons to be learned, a new cycle, luck, cause and effect, opportunity, destiny.
	Shadow: Resistance to change, being stuck in loops of ego, bad luck, reaping what you have sown, failure, a dead end, stagnation, setbacks.
Numerology:	10, 1 + 0 = 1
Astrology:	Jupiter
Justice (The judge/ manipulator archetype):	*Positive:* Disputes, legal matters, mediation, tribunals, fairness, balance, 'justice will be done', strategy, clear vision, contracts.
	Shadow: Injustice, losing a case, 'two wrongs don't make a right', the abuse of authority, being in the wrong, dishonesty, excess, loss, false accusations.
Numerology:	Master number 11, 1 + 1= 2
Astrology:	Libra
The Hanged Man (The sacrificial/martyr/seeker/ saint archetype):	*Positive:* Separation, things turned on their head, sacrifices, new perspectives on familiar terrain, enlightenment, flexibility, a crossroads.
	Shadow: Attachment to an old story, refusal to see another point of view, blinkered vision, martyrdom, futility, apathy, lack of fulfilment, depression.
Numerology:	12, 1 + 2 = 3
Astrology:	Neptune
Death (The transformer/ agent of change archetype):	*Positive:* Transformation, clutter clearing, starting afresh, the phoenix rising from the ashes, the reinvention of self, letting go of what no longer serves, transition, renewal, rebirth, purification.
	Shadow: Clinging to the old, refusal to change, being stuck, chronic clutter, mystery, inertia, decay, a standstill, fear of change, obstinacy
Numerology:	13, 1 + 3 = 4
Astrology:	Scorpio

Major Arcana Archetype	Key Attributes
Temperance (The mediator/adept/protector archetype):	*Positive:* Patience, a compromise, relaxation, moderation, healing, harmony, bringing things into balance, a win-win scenario, self-restraint.
	Shadow: A lack of discipline, toxic imbalances, excess, fanaticism, discord, wasted energy, inappropriate behaviour, immorality.
Numerology:	14, 1 + 4 = 5
Astrology:	Sagittarius
The Devil (The prostitute/ slave/manipulator/ controller/shadow archetype):	*Positive:* Desire, 'the ties that bind', addiction, the shadow side, owning the disowned aspects of self, the unconscious, ambition, bondage.
	Shadow: Negativity, greed, materialism, possessiveness, jealousy, controlling behaviour, obsession, fanaticism, co-dependency, the abuse of power.
Numerology:	15, 1 + 5 = 6
Astrology:	Capricorn
The Tower (The destroyer/ Kali/awakener archetype):	*Positive:* Bad news, shocks, the rug pulled out from underneath you, accidents, storms, living your truth, trauma, crisis management.
	Shadow: Injustice, depression, overreaction, the inability to deal with crisis, collapse, catastrophe, being overwhelmed, 'what you resist persists'.
Numerology:	16, 1 + 6 = 7
Astrology:	Mars
The Star (The optimist/ healer/humanitarian archetype):	*Positive:* Hope, inspiration, optimism, illumination, special talents, creativity, vitality, spiritual growth, blessings, altruism, luck, happiness, healing.
	Shadow: Ingratitude, victim mentality, focusing on what you don't want, delays, pessimism, disillusionment, anxiety, loss, ill health.
Numerology:	17, 1 + 7 = 8
Astrology:	Aquarius
The Moon (The grandmother/wise woman/ Maya archetype):	*Positive:* Intuition, dreams, hunches, the unconscious, creativity, the mother, integrity, imagination, being psychic, fantasy, wilderness.
	Shadow: Delusions, confusion, uncertainty, deception, betrayal, lying to yourself, hidden information, being gullible, depression, mood swings, doubt.
Numerology:	18, 1 + 8 = 9
Astrology:	Pisces

Major Arcana Archetype	Key Attributes
The Sun (The inner child/ father archetype):	*Positive:* Success, fulfilment, results, abundance, celebration, joy, a childlike attitude, generosity, radiance, zest, the achievement of goals, energy, empowerment.
	Shadow: Arrogance, childishness, alienation, laziness, egotism, narcissism, failure, delayed success, unhappiness, misjudgement.
Numerology:	19, 1 + 9 = 10, 1 + 0 = 1
Astrology:	The Sun
Judgement (The rebirth/ resurrection/judge archetype):	*Positive:* Evaluation, discernment, karma, overcoming old fears, analysis, rebirth, rejuvenation, cleansing, purification, metamorphosis.
	Shadow: Judging others, being sarcastic, being overly critical, the inner critic, self-pity, a victim mentality, discrimination, a forced ending, regret, the fear of death.
Numerology:	20, 2 + 0 = 2
Astrology:	Pluto
The World (The self-realization/individuation archetype):	*Positive:* Completion, reward, fulfilment, wholeness, self-actualization, elation, triumph, freedom, 'the world's your oyster'.
	Shadow: Delayed success, frustration, not finishing what you started, not being able to see the wood for the trees, imperfection, being stuck in a rut.
Numerology	21, 2 + 1 = 3
Astrology:	Saturn

Basic Numerology	Key Attributes
0	Pure potential, protection, 'anything is possible'.
1	**The Initiator:** Independent, dynamic, self-reliant, pioneering. A free thinker with original ideas and entrepreneurial spirit. Leadership. The father. The active male, yang principle.
2	**The Helper:** Union, relationships, a community-orientated outlook, a team player. Collaboration is key to success. An instinctive, sensitive, caring nature. The mother. The receptive female yin principle.
3	**The Entertainer:** Communication, humour, dynamism, growth, energy, imagination, creativity, self-expression. Enthusiasm, projects, lust for life. A lively, energetic extrovert who lives life to the full.
4	**The Planner:** Conservative, methodical, stable, pragmatic, practical. Tenacity, patience, conservatism, traditional values. A goal-orientated, grounded outlook. Foundations, building a legacy.

Basic Numerology	Key Attributes
5	**The Revolutionary:** Conflict, travel, passion, transformation, a tendency towards excess. A natural anarchist, an agent of change. Chaos, adventure, freedom, tests, learning.
6	**The Harmonizer:** Heart energy, love, beauty and calm. A natural host in service to the community who is charitable and understanding. Aesthetics, peace, reconciliation, accord, art, truth, justice, compassion, expansion.
7	**The Mystic:** Contemplation, reflection, meditation. A loner, psychic and intuitive, who is interested in health and has exacting standards and a tendency towards perfectionism. Philosophy, metaphysics, self-analysis, sensitivity.
8	**The Power Broker:** Deep reserves of personal strength, karma, evolution, responsibility, recognition, status, material rewards. Highly-developed judgement and discrimination. A mediator, generous and fair. Matters of life and death.
9	**The Universalist:** Compassion, self-awareness, enlightenment, the completion of a cycle. A friendly idealist, extremely well read, with a forgiving nature. A humanitarian and philanthropist. Tolerance, fulfilment, fortune, fate, selfless love.
Master Number: 11	**The Master Visionary:** The seer, prophet, psychic. Mysticism, the esoteric.
Master Number: 22	**The Master Builder:** The physical manifestation of visions. Planning for the future, the exoteric, structure and foundations.
Master Number: 33	**Christ Consciousness:** Perfect love, compassion, forgiveness, peace. Ultimate union. As above, so below.
Master Number: 44	**The Greater Good:** Building a legacy for future generations. Destiny, fate.

Basic Colours	Key Attributes
Black	The shadow, lack of identity, unacknowledged aspects of self, hidden fears, the unconscious. Night-time, winter, midnight. The dark night of the soul. Our hidden self. The absence of colour.
White	The crown chakra, spirituality, purity, innocence. Emotional cleansing, innocent endeavour, the Higher Self. The light at the end of the tunnel, the transition from life to death. Pure consciousness, awareness. All colours united.

Basic Colours	Key Attributes
Red	The root chakra, passion, romance, blood and violence. Danger, anger, heat, rashes. The physical aspect of sexuality, the 'hot-blooded male', the 'female on heat', the Earth, receiving and physical manifestation.
Orange	The sacral chakra, joy, optimism, creativity, hope, play, the psychology of sex. The psychology of prosperity, luck, abundance, trust, feelings.
Yellow	The solar-plexus chakra, will power, daytime, sunshine. Being positive, bright, optimistic. Doing what you need to do, taking action in the world. Knowing yourself. Standing up for yourself.
Green	The heart chakra, love, healing, emotions, relationships. A soothing, calming, relaxing approach. Growth, new beginnings, spring-like emergence. Compassion, openness, generosity, humility and gratitude.
Blue	The throat chakra, all forms of communication, arts, literature, writing, being free to express yourself. Languages, speaking your truth, not compromising.
Purple	The third-eye chakra, vision, inner 'knowing', clarity, intuition, dreams, instincts, hunches, imagination, ideas and inspiration.

Basic Elements	Key Attributes
Fire	Passion, vision, action, magnetism, charisma, warmth, spontaneity; burnout.
Earth	Solidity, nourishment, physical work, material abundance, foundations, structure, stability; stubbornness.
Wood	Growth, creativity, new ideas, projects; scattered energies, never completing anything, dead wood.
Water	Memory, the unconscious, emotions, intuition, dreams, independence, initiating; lack of focus, lack of boundaries.
Metal	Money, discipline, truth at all costs; being sharp, focused, controlling, conflict, battles, arguments, critical moments.
Ether	Spirit, the all that is, the basic state from which all phenomena arise, the zero-point field, the data stream, communication.

Basic Directions	Key Attributes (These are based on my knowledge of the Peruvian Cosmo vision; other systems vary in their directional attributes.)
North	Air, the sky, wind, spirit, communication. The father, the Great Mystery. The Higher Self. Relates to matters of the spiritual self: intuition, visions, prayers, self-realization and faith.
South	Earth, the planet, physical, roots. The mother. Relates to matters of the physical self and the physical world around us: structures, foundations, legacies, physical healing.
East	Fire, the sun, mind, vision. The conscious mind. Relates to matters of the intellectual self: ideas, decisions, choices, active imagination, beliefs, assumptions.
West	Water, the moon, emotions, memories. The unconscious mind. Relates to matters of the emotional self: feelings, past memories, unresolved emotions.

Further Reading and Resources

Further Reading

Steve Andreas and Connirae Andreas, PhD, 'A Brief History of NLP Timelines', *VAK International NLP Newsletter*, vol. 10, no. 1, Winter 1991–1992

Deirdre Barrett, PhD, *The Committee of Sleep*, Crown Publishers, 2001

William Bloom, *The Endorphin Effect*, Piatkus Books, 2001

Fraser Boa, *The Way of the Dream: Conversations on Jungian Dream Interpretation with Marie-Louise von Franz*, Shambhala, 1994

Carlos Castaneda, *The Art of Dreaming*, Thorsons, 1994

Theresa Cheung, *The Element Encyclopaedia of 20,000 Dreams,* HarperElement, 2006

Collaboration of 10 Authors, Wellcome Trust, *Sleeping and Dreaming*, Black Dog Publishing, 2007

Delia Cushway and Robyn Sewell, *Counselling with Dreams and Nightmares*, Sage Publications, 2001

Lorie Eve Dechar, *Five Spirits*, Lantern Books, 2006

Larry Dossey, MD, *Space, Time and Medicine*, Shambhala, 1982

A. E. I. Falconar, *How to Use Your Nous*, Non-Aristotelian Publishing, 1986

William V. Harris, *Dreams and Experience in Classical Antiquity*, Harvard University Press, 2009

Ernest L. Hartman, MD, *The Functions of Sleep*, Yale University Press, 1973

J. Allan Hobson, *Dreaming: A Very Short Introduction*, Oxford University Press, 2002

Ione, *Listening in Dreams*, iUniverse books, 2005

Tad James and Wyatt Woodsmall, *Time Line Therapy and the Basis of Personality*, Meta Publications, 1988

C. G. Jung, *Dreams*, Routledge Classics, 2002

Stephen LaBerge, *Lucid Dreaming*, Ballantine Books, 1985

Stephen LaBerge, and Howard Rheingold, *Exploring the World of Lucid Dreaming*, Ballantine Books, 1990

Alan Lightman, *Einstein's Dreams*, Warner Books, 1993

Chogyal Namkhai Norbu, *Dream Yoga and the Practice of Natural Light*, Snow Lion Publications, 1992

Tenzin Wangyal Rinpoche, *The Tibetan Yogas of Dream and Sleep*, Snow Lion Publications, 1998

John A. Sanford, *Dreams: God's Forgotten Language*, HarperCollins, 1989

Edward Tick, PhD, *The Practice of Dream Healing*, Quest Books, 2001

Merilyn Tunneshende, *Twilight Language of the Nagual*, Bear & Company, 2004

Montague Ullman, MD, and Nan Zimmerman, *Working with Dreams*, The Aquarian Press, 1987

Resources

You can find more details of my work, dream circles, workshops, talks and individual sessions on my website: www.thedreamwhisperer.com.

For regular dream updates, follow me on twitter@ dreamwhisperer, or to share dreams join my Facebook fan page, The Dream Whisperer.

Dream Essences

The specially commissioned Limelight Essence called 'Dream Fairies' that aids dream recall can be purchased from www. thedreamwhisperer.com or from Rosemary Hanson at www. limelightessences.co.uk.

Space Clearing

Nitraj incense and white sage smudge sticks can be purchased from www.thedreamwhisperer.com.

Geopathic Stress and EMFs

If you want to learn more, then the 'Radiofrequency, EMFs and Health Risks' article in the Powerwatch subscription section at www.powerwatch.org.uk has a detailed and up-to-date overview of the existing science on microwave frequency, EMFs and their effects on our health.

Helios plug-in environment harmonizer can be purchased from www.thedreamwhisperer.com.

Dulwich Health is a good resource for further information on geopathic stress and sells Raditech machines. See www.dulwichhealth.co.uk

Orchard Dect low-radiation phones can be found at www.lowradiation.co.uk.

For quartz phoneshields, see www.thedreamwhisperer.com.

For clear quartz and amethyst crystals, see www.thedreamwhisperer.com.

Artistic Solutions to *Feng Shui* Issues

For frosted panels from your own photographs for mirrored wardrobes, etc., contact Vahe Saboonchian, United Graphics, Unit 10, Wadsworth Business Centre, 21 Wadsworth Road, Perivale, Middlesex, UB6 7LQ; tel: 020 8997 6246; email: info@united-graphics.co.uk.

For beautiful *feng shui* artwork, see Carla Miles, tel: 0118 9669968; website: www.energeticart.co.uk.

Dowsing and Earth Acupuncture

You can purchase dowsing rods from www.thedreamwhisperer.com.

For more information on Earth acupuncture training and for a list of professional dowsers, see www.britishdowsers.org.

Autogenic Technique

For further information on this technique, see www.
goodmedicine.org.uk/goodknowledge/autogenic-relaxation-
training.

Colour Styling

Jules Standish, colour and style consultant, tel: 01403 822565;
website: www.colourconsultancy.co.uk; email: jules@
colourconsultancy.co.uk.

Moon calendar available from http://infra-azure.org/
main/?page_id=2

Notes

Notes

Notes

Notes

Notes

Notes

Notes

Hay House Titles of Related Interest

Ask and It Is Given, by Esther and Jerry Hicks

Ask Your Guides, by Sonia Choquette

Dreams & Beyond, by Madhu Tandan

Past, Present and Future, by David Wells

The Way of Wyrd, by Brian Bates